THE AT⊙WAR SERIES

B-17
AT WAR

BILL YENNE

ZENITH
PRESS

First published in 2006 by Zenith Press, an imprint of
MBI Publishing Company, Galtier Plaza, Suite 200, 380
Jackson Street, St. Paul, MN 55101-3885 USA

MBI Publishing Company titles are also available at dis-
counts in bulk quantity for industrial or sales-promo-
tional use. For details write to Special Sales Manager at
MBI Publishing Company, Galtier Plaza, Suite 200, 380
Jackson Street, St. Paul, MN 55101-3885 USA

ISBN-13: 978-0-7603-2522-3
ISBN-10: 0-7603-2522-7

Editors: Lindsay Hitch and Steve Gansen
Designer: Sara Grindle

Printed in China

        Library of Congress Cataloging-in-Publication Data

Yenne, Bill
  B-17 at war / Bill Yenne.
      p. cm.
  ISBN-13: 978-0-7603-2522-3
  ISBN-10: 0-7603-2522-7
  1. World War, 1939-1945--Aerial operations, American.
2. B-17 bomber--History. I. Title.
  D790.Y46 2006
  940.54'4973--dc22

On the cover: Main: B-17Gs of the 532nd Bombardment
Squadron of the 381st Bombardment Group en route to
the target, escorted by a P-51B "little friend." *USAAF via
National Archives*

   Inset: *NineONine* is a fully restored B-17G owned
and operated by the Collings Foundation of Stow,
Massachusetts. *Bill Yenne*

On the frontispiece: In this patriotic wartime illustration, a young lad and his grandfather ponder the power
and majesty of a formation of Boeing B-17E Flying
Fortresses taking off from a nearby U.S. Army air field.
Author collection

On the title pages: Gleaming silver B-17G Flying
Fortresses of the USAAF Eighth Air Force head out to
punish Adolf Hitler's Third Reich, escorted by a P-51B
Mustang fighter aircraft. These Forts were assigned to the
381st Bombardment Group, which was based at
Ridgewell in Essex from June 1943 until after Hitler had
been defeated and World War II ended in Europe. *USAAF
via National Archives*

About the Author:
Bill Yenne is the San Francisco–based author of more
than two dozen books on military, aviation, and historical
topics. He is a member of the American Aviation
Historical Society and the American Society of
Journalists & Authors, as well as a graduate of the
Stanford University Professional Publishing Course.
He is a regular contributor to *International Air Power
Review*. As the author of *Story of the Boeing Company*,
he is intimately acquainted with the B-17 and its
sister aircraft.

CONTENTS

ACKNOWLEDGMENTS

THE AUTHOR WISHES TO THANK MIKE LOMBARDI AND TOM LUBBESMEYER OF THE BOEING ARCHIVES for many years of assistance in researching and writing about Boeing aircraft. Important reference works that were invaluable in providing vital statistical data include *The Army Air Forces in World War II Combat Chronology*, compiled by Kit Carter and Robert Mueller and published by the Office of Air Force History in 1973, as well as Roger Freeman's many excellent works on the "Mighty" Eighth Air Force.

A close-up view of a Boeing B-17G shows one of the aircraft's Wright Cyclone radial engines and a Hamilton Standard propeller. The Flying Fortress has earned its place in the history of World War II, but she is also a beautiful piece of machinery and a milestone from the classic era of American industrial design. *Bill Yenne*

INTRODUCTION

THE BOEING B-17 FLYING FORTRESS WAS POSSIBLY THE GREATEST AMERICAN WARPLANE OF WORLD WAR II, and perhaps of all time. Almost any aviation historian would place it among the top half dozen on either list. It saw action at Pearl Harbor on the first morning of American involvement in the war, and it went on to be the key U.S. Army Air Forces (USAAF) weapon in carrying the war to Germany's industrial heartland. During World War II, the Boeing Airplane Company of Seattle earned the reputation of being one of the world's preeminent makers of four-engine strategic bombers, some of the key weapons systems responsible for the Allied victory over the Axis. Of the great Allied strategic bombers, Boeing built two of the most important: the B-17 Flying Fortress heavy bomber and the B-29 Superfortress very-heavy bomber. The latter, the larger brother of the B-17, arrived late in the war and carried the same message to the Japanese warlords that the B-17 had to Adolf Hitler.

The Flying Fortress formed the backbone of the great USAAF Eighth and Fifteenth Air Force air offensive against German-occupied Europe. B-17s dropped over six hundred forty thousand tons of bombs—roughly half of the overall total dropped by American bombers of all types—on Germany and German positions in occupied Europe. For more than two years, the Eighth Air Force launched several hundred B-17s almost daily from fields throughout southern England. By the end of the war, raids involving nearly a thousand B-17s were not uncommon. These attacks struck Germany's Ruhr industrial region, as well as major urban areas from Hamburg to Berlin to Munich. Meanwhile, Fifteenth Air Force B-17s were able to strike German targets in and around Munich and Vienna, as well as throughout eastern Europe. The USAAF raids crippled the German armaments industry and systematically destroyed the German Reichsbahn railroad network.

A total of 12,731 Flying Fortresses were built, mostly by Boeing in Seattle, making the type the second most extensively produced bomber in American history. Total B-17 production was exceeded in number only by the Flying Fortress' fellow World War II strategic bomber, the Consolidated B-24 Liberator, of which 18,482 were manufactured. The B-17 and B-24 were both four-engine heavy bombers, roughly the same size and designed and used for essentially identical missions. In the early days of the war, they operated side by side throughout the world, but by 1943, the USAAF chose to focus all of the Flying Fortresses against Germany, while the Liberators continued to operate in the Pacific as well as in the European and Mediterranean Theaters.

The B-17 became the icon of America's mighty counteroffensive against Hitler's Third Reich, visible almost continuously on the home front in countless newsreels and in widely shown government films, such as William Wyler's legendary 1944 documentary *Memphis Belle: A Story of a Flying Fortress*.

This book is an overview of the combat career of the B-17 Flying Fortress from its baptism of fire in 1941 through its final combat missions on the eve of Victory over Japan Day (VJ-Day) in 1945. It should also serve as a tribute to all the courageous airmen, many of whom paid the ultimate price, who flew the Forts to victory.

Above: This would have been the scene as the waist gunners of a B-17E, clad in fleece-lined leather high-altitude gear, defended their Flying Fortress from enemy attack. *Boeing*

Right: A B-17F Flying Fortress of the Eighth Air Force 95th Bombardment Group framed against the high altitude contrails of a vast stream of heavy bombers headed into Germany to strike a blow against Hitler's war machine. *USAAF via National Archives*

The first of thirty-nine B-17Bs, one of which is seen here, made its debut on June 27, 1939. Next came the similar B-17Cs. The first of thirty-eight of these made its inaugural flight on July 21, 1940, a week short of five years after that of the Boeing Model 299 series prototype. With improved armor and self-sealing fuel tanks, the B-17C was the first Flying Fortress variant to see combat with the USAAF. *Boeing*

The first loss of a Flying Fortress was the crash on takeoff of the original Model 299 prototype, informally known as "XB-17." It occurred at Wright Field during air corps evaluations on October 30, 1935. Veteran Boeing test pilot Les Tower was killed, but most of the men aboard survived. A gust lock—which prevents wind from moving an aircraft's elevators while on the ground—caused the crash when the ground crew failed to remove it before takeoff. *Boeing*

CHAPTER ONE

INTRODUCING AND BUILDING THE FLYING FORTRESS

THE B-17 FLYING FORTRESS was the product of a doctrine that took shape during the 1930s within the U.S. Army Air Corps (U.S. Army Air Forces after June 1941). This doctrine, known as strategic air power, called for the use of long-range bombers to strike deep into enemy territory to destroy the war-making capability at its origin. Strategic targets included factories, railroad hubs, and other infrastructure, such as petroleum refining and storage facilities. Strategic air power is distinct from tactical air power, which involves using warplanes to attack enemy troops and communication at or near the front lines.

The air corps was a subsidiary of the army, so tactical air power was favored by the army's leaders because it directly supported ground troops. The untested doctrine of strategic air power was a hard sell for its advocates within the air corps, but by the 1930s, the time had arrived. The road that led to the B-17 began in 1933, with the secret air corps program called "Project A." The idea was for a very large bomber with a range of five thousand miles. Various companies submitted proposals, and Boeing's XB-15 won the Project A contest over the Martin

XB-16. Problems arose with the XB-15 in the design stage, however, because nobody in the United States had yet built an aircraft so large. The XB-15 was impressive when it was completed for exactly the same reason. The flight deck was the size of the living room in a small house, larger than anything most air crews had ever seen. By the time that it made its first flight in 1937, the XB-15 had been bypassed by the progress of aviation technology in the form of the Boeing Model 299 Flying Fortress.

The Flying Fortress evolved from an air corps request for proposals that was somewhat more modest than Project A. Issued in July 1934, the solicitation asked plane makers to submit designs for a bomber with a one-ton bomb load, an air speed in excess of two hundred miles per hour, and a range in excess of two thousand miles. It was envisioned originally as a coastal defense aircraft capable of attacking enemy warships, rather than a bomber capable of attacking an enemy at great distances, as were the Project A bombers. Specifically, this new bomber was to be a multiengine aircraft. In those days, both two- and four-engine bombers were considered multiengine aircraft. Indeed, the only four-engine

An armada of Y1B-17s over New York City in 1938 during an air corps publicity tour that ultimately took them to South America, demonstrating their long-range capability. These aircraft were assigned to the 2nd Bombardment Group based at Langley Field in Virginia, the first air corps unit equipped with operational Flying Fortresses. *USAAF via National Archives*

bombers that the air corps had considered were the secret Project A bombers that were still on drawing boards. Douglas Aircraft Company would respond to the request with the twin-engine DB-1, and Boeing would return with the four-engine Model 299.

The aircraft was designed by a team of brilliant young engineers, notably Edward Curtis Wells, and built at the company's expense. The new Boeing Model 299 first flew on July 28, 1935, powered with four Pratt & Whitney R1690 Hornet engines. At the rollout, a journalist described the huge four-engine bomber as a "flying fortress." The phrase was quickly adopted as the aircraft's official name.

The U.S. Army Air Corps Engineering Division at Wright Field, Ohio, tested the Boeing-owned

USAAF B-17 INVENTORY
IN SELECTED MONTHS

1941
June: 144
December: 198

1942
June: 535
December: 1,239

1943
June: 2,460
December: 3,528

1944
June: 4,428
September: 4,552
December: 4,419

1945
March: 3,972
June: 3,692
December: 1,400

1946
June: 718
December: 512

1951 (U.S. Air Force)
June: 53
December: 0

This operational Boeing B-17C Flying Fortress wears a natural metal finish and standard prewar air corps markings, circa 1940. The gold-and-black arrowhead identifies the aircraft as being assigned to Wright Field. The stylish red-and-white rudder markings were still found on some air corps aircraft as late as 1941. *Boeing*

First flown on September 5, 1941, the Boeing B-17E introduced a redesigned tail, including a new rudder and a tail turret. The absence of defensive armament to adequately cover the aircraft from the rear was a major shortcoming of earlier Flying Fortress models. *USAAF via National Archives*

Model 299 under the unofficial XB-17 designation for nearly three months. In October 1935, the XB-17 crashed at Wright Field, fatally injuring veteran Boeing test pilot Les Tower and resulting in the deaths of several others. The cause was traced to faulty ground handling. The aircraft itself, however, had already received a glowing recommendation.

In January 1936, the air corps ordered thirteen service test Model 299B aircraft under the designation Y1B-17. These, and the subsequent production aircraft, would be powered by variations of the Wright Cyclone radial engine. The first Y1B-17 made its debut in December 1936, and a single Y1B-17A static test aircraft (Model 299F) was created. When it became a flyable airframe, it was redesignated as B-17A. There were thirty-nine B-17B (Model 299M) Flying Fortresses—with a redesigned nose and improved engines—ordered in 1938. Meanwhile, the air corps had ordered 133 Douglas DB-1s under the designation B-18.

When World War II began in Europe in 1939, the U.S. Army began planning for the long-range defense of the Western Hemisphere against possible Axis incursion. By now, evaluation of the Flying Fortress had indicated that it would be the key heavy bomber. In 1940, the air corps would order eighty Model 299H aircraft as B-17C and B-17D. All had more armor and armament than the B-17B, as well as self-sealing fuel tanks. The B-17D had extra crew armor. Twenty of the B-17Cs would be delivered to Britain's Royal Air Force in the autumn of 1940 under the designation Fortress Mk I. These were the first Model 299s to enter combat.

By 1941, there were 150 B-17Cs and B-17Ds in the inventory of the air corps, which became the U.S. Army Air Forces in June of that year. December 7, 1941, found a large number of the B-17s deployed to the areas where the enemy would first strike American forces: Hawaii and the Philippines. Most of those in Hawaii were badly mauled in the Pearl Harbor attack. The B-17s in the

Philippines rallied but were ineffectual in stemming the Japanese onslaught, and those Flying Fortresses that survived retreated to Australia.

As noted earlier, the four-engine B-17 and the B-24 heavy bombers were tasked principally with strategic missions during World War II. They were complemented by twin-engine medium and light bombers that flew mainly tactical missions. The primary medium bombers were the North American B-25 Mitchell and the Martin B-26 Marauder. The foremost light, or attack, bombers were the A-20 Havoc (known as "Boston" in British nomenclature) and the A-26 Invader, both built by Douglas Aircraft Company.

THE DEFINITIVE FLYING FORTRESSES

As early as 1940, it had become evident that a major flaw in the Flying Fortress was its lack of defensive armament in the tail. Guns bristled from its nose, waist, and belly, but it was a six-sided fortress with no guns on its most vulnerable side. With this in mind, Boeing developed the B-17E (Model 299O), which introduced the tail turret that would be standard in the rest of the production series. The B-17E was the first Flying Fortress to be produced in large numbers: 512 would be built, all at Boeing's Plant 2 in Seattle.

The B-17E was also the first Flying Fortress to see combat on a regular basis. B-17Es were deployed to Australia in early 1942, and in July 1942, they arrived in England to become the nucleus of the USAAF Eighth Air Force that would undertake the great strategic offensive against Germany.

The B-17F (Model 299P) was introduced in April 1942 with Wright R1820-97 Cyclone engines delivering 1,380 horsepower at twenty-five thousand feet. In addition to the new engines, armament included a ventral ball turret and a one-piece, plexiglass nose. The faceted nose of the earlier model had inhibited visibility, making the one-piece nose a welcome improvement. The gross weight limit of the B-17F was greatly increased over that of the B-17E, and extra eleven-hundred-gallon fuel tanks, called "Tokyo tanks," extended the range significantly. It had been planned to have some of the B-17E production taken over by the other manufacturers with surplus production capacity, but the B-17F superseded the B-17E, and the plan was implemented with the newer model instead. Over the course of the fifteen months that the B-17F was in production, 605 were built by the Douglas factories and another 500 by Lockheed Vega, all in Southern California. Meanwhile, Boeing's Plant 2 would roll out a staggering 2,300 B-17Fs.

Introduced in the autumn of 1943, the B-17G (also Model 299P) was the definitive Flying Fortress. It had the ball turret, the R1820-97 engines, and all of the other B-17F improvements, as well as a forward-firing Bendix

The USAAF received the first B-17F in May 1942. It was similar to the B-17E, but it had more powerful engines and a one-piece plexiglass nose. It was also the first Flying Fortress variant to be produced by a three-company pool of manufacturers. In addition to Boeing in Seattle, Lockheed-Vega built B-17Es in Burbank, and Douglas built them in Long Beach. The one pictured is a Long Beach Flying Fortress. *Courtesy Harry Gann*

BOEING B-17 FLYING FORTRESS INDIVIDUAL MODEL PRODUCTION TOTALS

(Unless otherwise noted, all B-17s were built by the Boeing Airplane Company at Boeing Plant 2, Boeing Field, Seattle, Washington.)

XB-17 (Model 299): 1 (Boeing-owned prototype)

Y1B-17 (Model 299B): 13 (one of which was later redesignated as B-17)

Y1B-17A (Model 299F): 1 (later redesignated as B-17A)

B-17B (Model 299M): 39

B-17C (Model 299H): 38 (including 20 that served the RAF as Fortress Mk I)

B-17D (Model 299H): 42

B-17E (Model 299O): 512 (including 45 that served the RAF as Fortress Mk IIA)

B-17F (Model 299P):

      2,300 (built by Boeing; including 20 that served the RAF as Fortress Mk II)

      605 (built by Douglas Aircraft Company at Long Beach, California)

      500 (built by Lockheed Vega at Burbank, California)

B-17G (also Model 299P):

      4,035 (built by Boeing; including 112 that served the RAF as Fortress Mk III/IIIA)

      2,395 (built by Douglas Aircraft Company at Long Beach, California)

      2,250 (built by Lockheed Vega at Burbank, California)

<u>Noteworthy Postwar Conversions:</u>

B-17H (formerly B-17G): 12 converted as lifeboat carriers

QB-17L, QB-17N, and QB-17P (formerly B-17G): several converted as target drones

DB-17P (formerly B-17): several converted as target drone directors

B-38 (formerly B-17E): 1 (experimental re-engining project)

B-40 (formerly B-17F): 21 converted

---

chin turret that made it a true Flying Fortress. The chin turret was critical because it could defend the aircraft from a frontal attack by enemy interceptors. The B-17G also typically carried a bomb load of six thousand to ninety-six hundred pounds. Again, both Douglas and Lockheed Vega were called upon to supplement Boeing production. The California companies produced 2,395 and 2,250, respectively, and 4,035 were built in Seattle.

OTHER FLYING FORTRESS VARIANTS

Two experimental Model 299 variants were the XB-38 and the XB-40. The XB-38 project was aimed at deter-mining whether inline engines would significantly improve Model 299 performance. In May 1943, one B-17E was experimentally fitted with four 1,425-horsepower Allison V1710-89 twelve-cylinder liquid-cooled engines. Performance did increase, but the single XB-38 was destroyed by fire in June before the tests were completed. With the Allison engines in great demand for the P-38 and P-40 fighters, and with the B-17F coming on line, it was considered unnecessary to divert production capability to an untested project, so the XB-38 program was canceled.

The XB-40 project was intended to create a much more heavily armed aircraft to serve as a gun platform

SPECIFICATIONS OF SELECTED B-17 MODELS

XB-17 (Model 299)
Wingspan: 103 feet, 9 3/8 inches
Length: 68 feet, 9 inches
Gross weight: 32,432 pounds
Top speed: 236 miles per hour
Cruising speed: 140 miles per hour
Range: 3,101 miles
Ceiling: 24,620 feet
Powerplant: Four 750-horsepower Pratt &
    Whitney S1EG Hornets
Bomb load: 4,800 pounds

B-17C (Model 299H)
Wingspan: 103 feet, 9 inches
Length: 67 feet, 11 inches
Gross weight: 38,320 pounds
Top speed: 323 miles per hour
Cruising speed: 250 miles per hour
Range: 3,400 miles
Ceiling: 37,000 feet
Powerplant: Four 1,000-horsepower Wright
    R182065 Cyclones
Bomb load: 4,000 pounds

B-17E (Model 299O)
Wingspan: 103 feet, 9 inches
Length: 73 feet, 10 inches
Gross weight: 53,000 pounds
Top speed: 317 miles per hour
Cruising speed: 210 miles per hour
Range: 3,300 miles
Ceiling: 36,600 feet
Powerplant: Four 1,000-horsepower Wright
    R182065 Cyclones
Bomb load: 4,000 pounds

B-17G (Model 299P)
Wingspan: 103 feet, 9 inches
Length: 74 feet, 4 inches
Gross weight: 65,000 pounds
Top speed: 287 miles per hour
Cruising speed: 150 miles per hour
Range: 3,750 miles
Ceiling: 35,600 feet
Powerplant: Four 1,200-horsepower Wright
    R182097 Cyclones
Bomb load: 9,600 pounds

to escort B-17 bombers. Lockheed Vega converted a B-17F, which was redesignated as XB-40, and twenty YB-40s followed. Though the specific armament varied from plane to plane, there were as many as thirty automatic weapons, ranging from .50-caliber machine guns in multiple turrets to 20mm and, in some cases, 40mm cannons mounted in the waist positions. The first mission flown with a YB-40 escort was against Saint-Nazaire in May 1943, and there were others to follow. It soon became evident that while the B-40s could keep up with the bomb-laden B-17s on the way to the target, they could not, with the weight of all their guns and ammunition, match the speed and altitude of the empty B-17s on their way home. The project was deemed a failure and the program ended in August 1943. Four YB-40s would see service stateside as TB-40 crew trainers. The YB-40 chin turret was made standard in the B-17G.

Meanwhile, several B-17s were converted to transport aircraft under the designation C-108. The most famous C-108 was the *Bataan*, General Douglas MacArthur's executive transport. Another group of forty-seven B-17Gs and a B-17E were transferred to the U.S. Navy and U.S. Coast Guard, equipped with radar and used for patrol and search-and-rescue duties under the designation PB-1.

Deliveries of the "ultimate" Flying Fortress, the B-17G, began in September 1943. The armament was enhanced by the addition of the chin turret. The early B-17Gs, such as the one seen here, were delivered in standard dark green camouflage paint, but by mid-1944, they were left in natural metal finish. By 1944, the USAAF had decided that camouflage was no longer necessary for Eighth Air Force heavy bombers. Not painting them saved time and money, as well as weight and drag. This translated to higher cruising speed and a slightly greater payload capacity. *USAAF via National Archives*

THE NORDEN BOMBSIGHT

Of the many components that made up the B-17, there was no single piece of equipment that contributed more to its effectiveness as a precision bombing platform than the legendary Norden bombsight. During World War II, the USAAF trained more than forty-five thousand bombardiers and entrusted them with a weapon that they were sworn to secrecy to protect.

Bombardiers faced the task of aiming ordnance from vehicles traveling several hundred miles per hour, often bouncing up and down and sideways at the same time. Surface gunnery delivers a projectile that has its own momentum, while aerial bombs are propelled at a much slower speed, pulled toward their targets only by gravity. Thus, bombs are much more susceptible to the whims of wind currents that often flow in opposite directions at different altitudes and change speed and direction invisibly.

Even today, with the computing power of microelectronics, creating a calculating bombsight would be a complex task. But in the years between World War I and World War II, bombsight development was literally a hit-or-miss proposition.

The person who created the most sophisticated aiming device in history that did not use electronics was a man named Carl Lukas Norden. In 1911, he joined the research and development staff at the Sperry Gyroscope Company, where he would be recognized as a pioneer in the field of gyroscopically stabilized naval gun platforms. He resigned from Sperry in 1915 to strike out on his own, using his contacts within the U.S. Navy Bureau of Ordnance to line up work.

Ironically, the weapon that would account for the greatest offensive successes of the USAAF in World War II was created for the U.S. Navy. Because of his past performance on gyro stabilization, Norden was asked to develop a bombsight for the navy for hitting maneuvering warships from the air.

Norden began work in 1921 and delivered his Mk III model two years later. Ten years later, Norden had worked his way up to the Mk IV, a sophisticated gyro-optical device with a timing mechanism to tell the bombardier when to release the bombs. Provisions would be made to allow the bombardier to take lateral control of the aircraft from the pilot in order to line up the sight for the bomb run. Accuracy continued to improve, culminating with the Norden M-Series bombsight, delivered to the USAAF after 1943. If used correctly, it was capable of dropping bombs within a fifty-foot radius of its target from an altitude of over twenty thousand feet. This provided a level of precision up to eight times that of the contemporary British Mk XIV bombsight. In 1943, it was estimated that the Royal Air Force was able to put 5 percent of its bombs within one mile of the aiming point under combat conditions. By contrast, the USAAF Eighth Air Force was believed to be able to put 24 percent of its bombs to within one thousand yards of their targets. By 1944, using the Norden M-Series, the USAAF was able to drop 40 percent to within five hundred yards.

Later in the war, the Norden would be augmented by radar bombing systems to accurately drop ordnance through cloud cover and overcast conditions. These systems included Gee-H, H2X (codenamed "Mickey"), and Oboe, a system with a three-hundred-mile range.

THE USAAF NUMBERED AIR FORCES

The vast majority of the Flying Fortresses that engaged in combat during World War II served with the U.S. Army Air Forces. The primary exceptions were the few

This group of natural metal B-17Gs was photographed on July 15, 1944, during a training mission out of Laredo, Texas. By that time, large and ever-growing numbers of B-17Gs in Europe were blasting the Germans from one end of the continent to the other. The aircraft in the foreground is a Block 60 B-17G that was built in Seattle. *USAAF via National Archives*

that were used by Britain's Royal Air Force. The USAAF was created on June 20, 1941, as the operational successor organization to the U.S. Army Air Corps. In September 1947, the USAAF became independent of the army as the U.S. Air Force. During World War II, the USAAF was the largest air force in history, with more than seventy thousand aircraft and a personnel strength of over 2.3 million. As the plural in "U.S. Army Air Forces" implies, the USAAF was composed of multiple numbered air forces. In order to understand the operations of the USAAF during World War II, it is useful to have a brief sketch of the sixteen air forces active in World War II.

Originally, the USAAF designated the numbered air forces with a numeral, but it began designating them with a word on September 18, 1942, making the USAAF air forces equivalent to the army's numbered land armies. For the sake of clarity, the numbered air forces are referred to by their word throughout this book. The numbered air forces often contained subsidiary air commands, such as bomber commands, fighter commands, and others. These were designated with Roman numerals that matched the number of the parent air force.

In 1940, the four original numbered air forces were created within the continental United States (known as the "Zone of the Interior"). These four were originally four geographical air districts and were redesignated with numbers in April 1941. The First Air Force was originally the Northeast Air District, the Second Air Force was established as the Northwest Air District, the Third Air Force was originally the Southeast Air District, and the Fourth Air Force started as the Southwest Air District. Early in World War II, a few B-17s served briefly with each numbered air force, tasked with coastal patrol, but these operations were phased out in 1942, except on the East and Gulf Coasts, where a handful of B-17s were retained for antisubmarine patrols through much of the war.

The Sixth Air Force originated as the Panama Canal Air Force in October 1940 and was redesignated as the Sixth in September 1942. As with the four Zone-of-the-Interior air forces, the Sixth used a few B-17s in coastal patrol and antisubmarine operations early in the war, but these Flying Fortresses were replaced by other types by the end of 1943.

The Fifth Air Force was established as the Philippine Department Air Force in August 1941, redesignated as the Far East Air Force in October 1941 and as the Fifth Air Force in February 1942. During World War II, it functioned as the USAAF operational presence in the Southwest Pacific.

The Seventh Air Force was the counterpart of the Fifth in the Central Pacific. It originated as the Hawaiian Air Force in 1940 and was redesignated as the Seventh in February 1942.

The Thirteenth Air Force was activated in January 1943 as the third USAAF air force in the Pacific, equivalent to the Fifth and Seventh but serving in the South Pacific. Based consecutively on the rugged islands of New Caledonia, Espiritu Santo, and Guadalcanal, the Thirteenth was nicknamed the "Jungle Air Force." The Fifth, Seventh, and Thirteenth operated B-17s early in the war but phased them out by the fall of 1943, as the USAAF diverted the Flying Fortress fleet to the European Theater.

The Eighth Air Force was by far the largest user of B-17s ever, with twenty-seven bombardment groups operational with the Flying Fortress. The Eighth was created in February 1942 as the initial USAAF operational organization for activities in the European Theater. It absorbed the month-old VIII Bomber Command, which is considered to be its predecessor unit. The Eighth Air Force was transferred to the Pacific after the defeat of Germany in May 1945, but Japan surrendered before it became operational there. After the war, the Eighth was assigned to the Strategic Air Command, and it continued to operate strategic bombers through the end of the twentieth century.

The Ninth Air Force functioned as the USAAF tactical air force in the European Theater as the counterpart of the strategic Eighth Air Force. It was formed as an air support command in 1941, becoming the Ninth Air Force in April 1942. It went overseas to the eastern Mediterranean in November 1942, moved to England in October 1943, and to France in September 1944. In its early days, the Ninth operated a few B-17s, but as a tactical air force, it was mainly composed of fighters and medium, or smaller, bombers.

The Tenth Air Force was created in February 1942 for air combat operations in India and Burma. Only an occasional B-17 served with the Tenth.

The Eleventh Air Force originated in 1941 as the Air Field Forces of the Alaskan Defense Command, later designated as the Alaskan Air Force. It became the Eleventh in February 1942. The few B-17s assigned to the force when the war started conducted patrol operations. During the year beginning in June 1942, when the Japanese occupied the Aleutian Islands of Attu and Kiska, B-17s conducted raids from bases in Alaska. By the end of 1943, most Flying Fortresses had departed Alaska.

The Twelfth Air Force was activated in August 1942 for European Theater operations in England, but it was relocated to the western Mediterranean in November 1942 to participate in the Operation Torch invasion of North Africa. It remained in the Mediterranean through the end of the war. The Twelfth used B-17s in its early days, but after the activation of the strategic Fifteenth Air Force in 1943, it became the Fifteenth's tactical partner in the same relationship that the Ninth had with the Eighth Air Force.

The Fourteenth Air Force, successor to the earlier China Air Task Force (CATF), was created in March 1943 for operations in China. It was a companion to the Tenth Air Force as a component of the U.S. Army forces in the China-Burma-India (CBI) Theater. By the time the Fourteenth was born, the B-17 fleet had been fully earmarked for operations against Germany, not Japan.

The Fifteenth Air Force was activated in November 1943 as the Mediterranean Theater Strategic Air Force, the Mediterranean equivalent of the Eighth Air Force. It was the second largest operator of B-17s, with five bombardment groups using Flying Fortresses.

The Sixteenth through Nineteenth Air Forces were not activated during World War II.

The Twentieth Air Force was created in April 1944 as a strategic bombardment force for operations against Japan. It was equipped exclusively with the B-29 Superfortress very-heavy bomber—the big brother of the B-17 heavy bomber—and it was the only operational USAAF air force to operate B-29s during World War II. As such, it never operated B-17s.

By the time that the United States entered World War II, many of the early B-17B, B-17C, and B-17D aircraft that were in service with the USAAF had been painted in camouflage green and gray. *Boeing*

This 38th Reconnaissance Squadron B-17C is a victim of the December 7, 1941, attack on Pearl Harbor. Captain Raymond Swenson was piloting the aircraft, inbound to Hawaii from Hamilton Field north of San Francisco, when he ran into the attack. The Flying Fortress was hit by cannon fire from Japanese fighters, and a box of flares ignited within the fuselage. Swenson managed to get his burning aircraft to the ground at Hickam Field, adjacent to Pearl Harbor, but the aft section broke off as he touched down. *USAAF via National Archives*

CHAPTER TWO

B-17 OPERATIONS IN 1941

THE COMBAT CAREER OF THE Flying Fortress began, inauspiciously, five months before the United States entered World War II. Britain's Royal Air Force had begun taking delivery of its first aircraft in the spring of 1941. These planes, designated as Fortress Mk I, were the equivalent of the B-17C in USAAF nomenclature. On July 8, fifty-one Fortresses flew their debut high-altitude bombing missions with No. 90 Squadron of the RAF Bomber Command. This mission, targeting the German port of Wilhelmshaven, was a serious disappointment, as twenty-seven of the Fortresses had to abort for mechanical reasons, and because crews were not fully acclimated to their Fortresses. Additional RAF missions flown through late September against German naval targets were also discouraging because of difficulties with precision aiming from altitudes and vulnerability to Luftwaffe interceptors attacking from the rear. These two problems would be resolved with the introduction of the Norden bombsight and the tail turret that was standard on the B-17E and later models. However, the RAF made the decision in the fall of 1941 not to use the Fortress for large-scale strategic bombing.

After their unfavorable beginning, the RAF reassigned its Fortress Mk Is from Bomber Command to Coastal Command. For the most part, RAF Fortresses would spend the rest of the war flying coastal patrols and reconnaissance missions, although a few were tasked with special operations missions, such as radar jamming. During the war, small numbers of Fortresses would also serve nine RAF squadrons.

On December 7, 1941, the Japanese attack on Pearl Harbor, Hawaii, brought the United States into World War II. The USAAF B-17s had their baptism of fire during the Pearl Harbor attack, as a half dozen Flying Fortresses from the 38th Reconnaissance Squadron (Heavy), inbound from Hamilton Field, California, arrived in the airspace over Oahu as it swarmed with Japanese fighters. These aircraft—four B-17Cs and a pair of B-17Es—were shot at, but all managed to land without crashing, although one set down on a golf course. Also under attack by the Japanese was the USAAF's Hickam Field, which was immediately adjacent to the Pearl Harbor naval base. There were a dozen B-17Ds of the 5th Bombardment Group (Heavy) on the ground there, and eight were destroyed.

The formal declaration of war against Japan came on December 8 and against Germany on December 11. The United States and its B-17s were at war.

A B-17E proudly displays its army affiliation. It has been suggested that the principal audience for this feature of USAAF markings in late 1941 was the crew of U.S. Navy ships. Coincidentally, a view similar to this was featured on the cover of the December 1, 1941, issue of *Life* magazine, which was on American coffee tables at the time of the Pearl Harbor attack. *USAAF via National Archives*

As of December 7, the USAAF B-17 force numbered fewer than two hundred aircraft. These were assigned to the bomber commands of the four numbered air forces and three overseas commands. They served with both bombardment squadrons and with long-range reconnaissance squadrons contained within bombardment groups. The B-17 outfits within I Bomber Command included the squadrons assigned to the 2nd Bombardment Group (Heavy) at Langley Field, Virginia; the 34th Bombardment Group (Heavy) at Westover Field, Massachusetts; and the 43rd Bombardment Group (Heavy) at Dow Field, Maine.

Within the II Bomber Command, B-17s were assigned to the 39th Bombardment Group (Heavy) at Geiger Field, Washington. The III Bomber Command had B-17s within the 29th Bombardment Group (Heavy) at MacDill Field, Florida, and the 30th Bombardment Group (Heavy) at New Orleans Army Air Base.

The IV Bomber Command contained B-17s assigned to the 7th Bombardment Group (Heavy) of the 1st Bombardment Wing at Tucson, Arizona. This group and its constituent B-17 squadrons—the 9th, 11th, and 14th Bombardment Squadrons (Heavy), as well as the 38th and 88th Reconnaissance Squadrons (Heavy)—were en route to the Philippines via Hamilton Field and Hickam Field.

Meanwhile, within the Caribbean Defense Command's Caribbean Air Force, the VI Bomber Command had the 7th Reconnaissance Squadron (Heavy) at Howard Field, Panama Canal Zone, and the 44th Reconnaissance Squadron (Heavy) at Atkinson Field, British Guiana, both equipped with B-17s.

In the Pacific, the Hawaiian Air Force's 18th Bombardment Wing and 11th Bombardment Group (Heavy) at Hickam Field had B-17s assigned. In the Philippines, the V Bomber Command of the Far East Air Force (FEAF) contained the 19th Bombardment Group (Heavy) at Clark Field, which had two bombardment squadrons equipped with B-17s, not counting those transitioning from the IV Bomber Command in the United States to overseas units. Two additional B-17 squadrons, the 32nd Bombardment Squadron (Heavy) and the 38th Reconnaissance Squadron (Heavy), were en route to the Pacific via Hamilton Field and Hawaii. In the wake of the Pearl Harbor attack, the air echelons of these two squadrons were ordered to remain at Hickam to conduct reconnaissance missions around the Hawaiian Islands. A follow-up attack on Pearl Harbor was expected, but the Japanese carrier force had withdrawn. Additional B-17s reached Hawaii later in the month.

As the war began, the USAAF tasked the First and Fourth Air Forces with the air defense on the East and West Coasts of the United States. For the I and IV Bomber Commands, this meant overwater reconnaissance with all available aircraft to intercept any hostile naval forces that might approach the coasts. The bombers also began flying antisubmarine patrols. Eventually, this task would rest mainly with obsolescent B-18s and other types, but in December 1941 and through much of 1942, it included B-17s as well. On the West Coast, Flying Fortress patrols were conducted from Muroc Army Air Base (now Edwards Air Force Base) in California and Geiger Field, Washington, for several weeks. On the East Coast, Flying Fortresses would be used for ocean patrol duties until October 1942. These operations were conducted out of Westover

The standard color scheme for USAAF aircraft early in World War II included dark olive green upper surfaces and dark gray below. After deployment, especially in theaters with harsh sun, the green faded to a color resembling the khaki of the airmen's uniforms. Early in 1942, the red center of the national insignia was deleted to avoid possible confusion with the Japanese rising sun insignia, known to the Allies informally as the "meatball." *Boeing*

Field, Massachusetts; Mitchel Field, New York; Langley Field, Virginia; Pope Field, North Carolina; and MacDill Field, Florida, as well as briefly from Dow Field, Maine.

Across the International Dateline, where it was December 8 when the Pearl Harbor attack occurred, the Japanese conducted air attacks against the Philippines a few hours later. Word of Pearl Harbor had already reached the Philippines and the FEAF, under the command of Major General Lewis Brereton. It was here that the Flying Fortresses would begin their first sustained combat operations. There were thirty-five B-17s in the Philippines, sixteen of them at Del Monte Field on the island of Mindanao and nineteen at Clark Field near Manila on the island of Luzon. The latter were ordered to get airborne to prevent being caught on the ground and to patrol the waters around Luzon. Unfortunately, many were back on the ground to refuel when the Japanese attacked, and most were destroyed.

On December 9, patrols resumed using the few surviving B-17s, and, on December 10, the USAAF Flying Fortresses conducted their first offensive bombing missions. They struck a convoy landing troops and equipment on Luzon, and Captain Colin Kelly of the 14th Bombardment Squadron attacked and reportedly sank the battleship *Haruna*. Kelly was shot down by fighters as he returned to Clark Field and was later posthumously awarded the Distinguished Service Cross. In fact, the warship was the heavy cruiser *Ashigara*, and it did not sink. On December 14, B-17 pilot Lieutenant Hewitt Wheless earned the Distinguished Service Cross for an attack on the enemy invasion fleet.

On December 17, some of the surviving B-17s based in the southern Philippines were withdrawn to Batchelor Field near Darwin, Northern Territory, in Australia. On Christmas Day, the FEAF V Bomber Command would formally reestablish its headquarters at Darwin. The command would regroup there for offensive actions against the Japanese invasion of the Philippines, as well as the invasion of the Netherlands East Indies (now Indonesia), mainly the island of Java. On December 22, B-17s from Batchelor Field attacked Japanese ships in Davao Bay off Mindanao Island and landed to refuel at Del Monte.

That same day, Prime Minister Winston Churchill arrived in Washington, D.C., for the Anglo-American Arcadia summit to plan war strategy with President Franklin Roosevelt and American and British Chiefs of Staff. At this historic meeting, they would create the Combined Chiefs of Staff positions to direct the war effort, and would decide to put their principal military efforts in the war against Germany, while merely containing the Japanese offensive until Germany was on the defensive. It was a global war with a global strategy in which the Flying Fortress was a key weapon.

In the wee hours of December 23, four B-17s from Del Monte bombed the Japanese invasion fleet in Lingayen Gulf, Luzon. On Christmas Eve, they struck enemy shipping at Davao and returned to Batchelor Field. By this time, American ground forces on Luzon had been overwhelmed by the invaders and were withdrawing into defensive positions on the Bataan Peninsula. Things would get worse for the Americans in the Pacific during the early months of the new year—much worse.

A B-17E Flying Fortress in dark olive green as delivered from the Seattle factory in early 1942 with USAAF markings. *Author collection*

Boeing B-17E Flying Fortresses head to war in early 1942. The British-style tricolor rudder patch was seen on many USAAF aircraft that were operational in the Middle East and North Africa in 1942 and early 1943. Some of these B-17s were brought from the Pacific Theater in 1942 by General Lewis Brereton. *Author collection*

CHAPTER THREE

B-17 OPERATIONS IN 1942

THE PACIFIC THEATER OF OPERATIONS

When the Arcadia conference wrapped up in Washington on January 14, 1942, President Roosevelt, Prime Minister Churchill, and their military staffs had decided to conduct a major offensive against Germany while containing Japan. However, except for British actions in North Africa, little would or could be done against German forces until late in the year. The Japanese onslaught in the Pacific, meanwhile, raged like wildfire. They had captured Hong Kong and most of the Philippines, and were swarming through Malaya, the East Indies, and the islands of the South Pacific. Australia, too, was threatened.

In the Pacific, the tiny handful of B-17s was the only long-range bomber force available to the Allies. The Flying Fortress operations in the Pacific Theater were important throughout the first full year of the war in that area, and limited operations were conducted using B-17s in the adjacent China-Burma-India (CBI) Theater during the early months of 1942.

Administratively, the Allied military commanders viewed the Pacific as three areas: the South Pacific (SOPAC), containing island chains such as the Solomons; the Southwest Pacific, including New Guinea; and the Central Pacific, or Pacific Ocean Area, which contained island chains such as the Marianas and Japan itself. For the USAAF, the Southwest Pacific was home to the Far East Air Force, which was redesignated Fifth Air Force on February 5, 1942. The Central Pacific was assigned to the Hawaiian Air Force, which became the Seventh Air Force on February 5, 1942. USAAF assets in the South Pacific area would operate closely with U.S. Navy and Marine Corps aviation units and would be under the direct control of the Joint Chiefs of Staff until the creation of the Thirteenth Air Force early in 1943.

In the CBI Theater, USAAF assets would soon fall under the newly created Tenth Air Force but would later be divided between the Tenth (India and Burma) and the Fourteenth (China).

At Arcadia, Roosevelt and Churchill also announced the creation of a unified command in the Southwest Pacific, with General Sir Archibald Wavell as supreme commander of American, British, Dutch, and Australian forces in that area.

On the first day of January 1942, B-17 operations got under way as Flying Fortress units, including the 93rd

Nose art had not yet evolved to the levels of artistic perfection that would be reached later in World War II. A group of GIs load practice bombs into a B-17E for a training mission from Ephrata Army Airfield in central Washington state, circa 1942. Early in the war, combat crews received both flight and gunnery training at Ephrata, which was just a short distance by air from Boeing Field, where the B-17Es were built. *Author collection*

Bombardment Squadron (Heavy), began moving north from Batchelor Field to airfields at Singosari and Malang on the island of Java, Palembang on Sumatra, and Kendari on Celebes (now Sulawesi) Island. Later in the month, bombers at Singosari moved on to Jogjakarta.

On January 5 and 9, Java-based B-17s went into action against Japanese ships in Davao Bay on Mindanao Island in the Philippines. On January 11, B-17s out of Malang struck Japanese landing forces on Tarakan Island off Borneo. Four days later, Palembang-based B-17s hit Sungei Patani Airfield in Malaya. On January 17, Malang-based B-17s staged through Kendari to bomb Langoan Airfield and ships in Menado Bay.

Additional B-17s were brought into the theater via Africa and India, but as the Japanese established a fighter base on Java, the losses were too severe and the practice was abandoned on January 20. The surviving Flying Fortresses soldiered on, and by February, replacement B-17s were coming into the theater by way of the Pacific Ocean.

Between January 22 and February 3, Malang-based B-17s were launched on more than fifteen missions against enemy shipping moving through Makassar Strait between Borneo and Celebes. Four ships sank. On January 28, Java-based B-17s struck airfields at Kendari on Celebes Island and Kuala Lumpur, Malaya.

Meanwhile, in late January, Hawaiian (Seventh) Air Force B-17s were deployed to operate with Joint Task Group 8.9 via Canton Island in the Phoenix Islands and Fiji. These were the first USAAF patrol operations conducted over vast areas in the Pacific, and they identified lessons in navigation and maintenance that needed to be learned for future operations.

On February 19, B-17s operating out of Malang and Jogjakarta began a series of strikes against Japanese ships landing troops on Bali that lasted until March 1. By this time, the Japanese presence in the Netherlands East Indies had become so strong that the Fifth Air Force withdrew all of its aircraft from Java. By March 2, they had all pulled back to bases in Australia.

By March, the situation in the Philippines had also deteriorated. The Japanese had pushed the American and Filipino defenders back into a narrow defensive perimeter on the Bataan Peninsula. The decision came to evacuate General Douglas MacArthur, the U.S. commander in the Philippines. In the dark of night, he was taken to Mindanao by a U.S. Navy PT boat; from there he was flown to Australia in a B-17E on March 17. For the rest of the war, MacArthur's executive aircraft would be a modified B-17E, redesignated as C-108 and nicknamed *Bataan*. On April 18, MacArthur was placed in command of all Allied forces in the Southwest Pacific. A week after MacArthur was evacuated, three B-17s of the 40th Reconnaissance Squadron (Heavy), 19th Bombardment Group (Heavy), brought Philippine President Manuel Quezon and his family to Australia. The Bataan Peninsula fell to the Japanese on April 9, and on May 6, the last organized American resistance within the Philippines collapsed with the capture of the island fortress of Corregidor.

Looking over the bombardier's right shoulder in a B-17E on a mission somewhere over the Pacific Ocean. The faceted plexiglass nose of the B-17E was superseded by the B-17F's standard one-piece, which entered service during the summer of 1942. *Author collection*

One of the most famous Flying Fortresses was *The Swoose*, tail number 40-3097, seen here late in the war, marked with the flags of places it visited during its colorful career. The B-17D was delivered in April 1941 and was based in the Philippines when the Japanese attacked. The aircraft flew numerous missions against the Japanese, including the first USAAF night bombing of World War II. The B-17D was flown to Australia early in 1942, and its battle damage was repaired. Her new pilot, Captain Weldon Smith, named her *The Swoose* because the repaired Flying Fortress contained parts of two airplanes. The reference was to a then-popular song about a "funny-looking gander" that was part swan and part goose. Later, Captain Frank Kurtz took over, using the plane to transport Lieutenant General George Brett, the commander of Allied Air Forces in Australia. In August 1942, Kurtz flew Brett to the United States, breaking a speed record, and later to Panama. Kurtz liked the plane so much that in 1944 he named his newborn daughter after it. Swoosie Kurtz later became a well-known actress. After the war, Kurtz bought *The Swoose* for $350. The city of Los Angeles planned to use the plane in a memorial, but the idea faded and the plane was passed around to several owners, ending up in storage at the National Air & Space Museum's Paul Garber restoration facility at Silver Hill, Maryland. *Colonel O. C. Griffith via David Menard*

Meanwhile, in India on March 5, the newly created Tenth Air Force was placed under the command of former FEAF boss Major General Lewis Brereton, who had arrived from the Netherlands East Indies ten days earlier. His command consisted of just eight B-17s. Three days later, their initial mission in the CBI Theater was carrying 474 troops and twenty-nine tons of supplies from India to Burma and returning with 423 civilians. On March 12, the 7th Bombardment Group (Heavy) and 88th Reconnaissance Squadron (Heavy) would relocate to Karachi (then part of India, now part of Pakistan). Operational B-17 missions against targets in Burma would be flown from Dum Dum in India.

The first CBI bombing mission, led by Brereton himself, came on the night of April 2. Three B-17s attacked shipping in the Andaman Islands off the southern coast of Burma, reportedly hitting a cruiser and a transport. On April 3, six B-17s from Asansol, India, bombed warehouses and docks at Rangoon, Burma, starting three large fires. Additional Flying Fortress raids on Rangoon followed on April 16, April 28, and May 9, with attacks on Mingaladon Airfield in Burma on May 5, 6, and 9.

The most important strategic bombing mission in the Pacific during 1942 came on April 18, and it involved not B-17s, but B-25s. On April 18, sixteen of these medium bombers were daringly launched from the aircraft carrier USS *Hornet*. Under the command of General Jimmy Doolittle, the B-25s conducted the first USAAF raid against the Japanese heartland, striking Tokyo, Kobe, Yokohama, and Nagoya. The damage done was negligible, but the morale boost in the United States was enormous. Doolittle would later move to England to command the largest USAAF B-17 force in the world.

In May, it was the U.S. Navy's turn to make headlines, battling the Imperial Japanese Navy in the Battle of the Coral Sea north of Australia and preventing them from landing troops at Port Moresby on New Guinea. The Coral Sea was seen as an important strategic victory for the Allies because it prevented the Japanese from making an amphibious landing on the south side of New Guinea. This would have placed them within easy striking distance of Australia. The Japanese already had forces at Lae on the north side of New Guinea, and they would continue to battle Australian and American ground troops in the intractable mountains and jungles to reach Port Moresby by land.

A cluster of what appear to be incendiary bombs tumble from the bomb bay of a B-17F over an enemy target. *USAAF via National Archives*

Against this backdrop, one of the principal missions of the Fifth Air Force B-17s, for as long as Flying Fortresses were in the theater, would be against the Japanese bases at Lae and elsewhere in New Guinea. Also high on the Fifth Air Force B-17 target list until the summer of 1943 would be the huge Japanese naval base at Rabaul on the neighboring island of New Britain. Both of these campaigns began soon after the Battle of the Coral Sea. On May 13, 14, 22, and 25, 1942, Flying Fortresses flew missions against Rabaul. Lae would be a target on May 14, 16, and 31. On May 18, B-17s struck shipping in Kupang Bay off Timor Island, west of New Guinea.

Back in the CBI, May continued to be a big month for Tenth Air Force B-17s. Three times between May 12 and May 16, and again on May 29 and 30, Dum Dum–based B-17s attacked the airfield at Myitkyina, Burma. The base, captured by the Japanese, posed a serious threat to the Allied base at Dinjan. On the first of June, a bomber raid against the Rangoon dock and harbor area sank a tanker and left another listing. Another raid on Rangoon followed on June 4, but for much of the month, heavy bombers were grounded by monsoons. On June 26, General Brereton was transferred to the Middle East

Theater, taking the aircraft and crews of the 9th Bombardment Squadron (Heavy) and leaving the Tenth Air Force largely depleted of offensive assets. When the heavy bomber force in the CBI was built up later, the heavy bombers were almost exclusively B-24s, as B-17s would be concentrated in Europe after 1943.

Also in June 1942, attention in the Pacific Theater again shifted to naval actions, this time north of Hawaii to a battle that would have been decisive regardless of the outcome. As it was, the Japanese lost. They lost big, and they lost four irreplaceable aircraft carriers. Fought on June 4, the Battle of Midway was the decisive naval battle of the Pacific Theater of World War II. The Japanese had hoped to occupy Midway Island, north of the Hawaiian Islands, as well as Attu and Kiska Island in the Aleutian Islands west of Alaska. They failed with Midway but succeeded in the Aleutians on June 6 and 7. In any case, the actions that week put the Imperial Japanese Navy on the defensive and marked the high point of Japanese territorial expansion.

B-17s were not without a role in these momentous events, although it was a small role. The Seventh Air Force sent B-17s to Midway from Hawaii at the end of May

A later-model B-17F from Boeing production Block 80 makes a pass over Washington's Mount Rainier on its delivery flight out of Boeing Field in Seattle. The numeral "2" at the beginning of the tail number identifies it as an aircraft ordered in 1942. *Boeing*

when word of the Japanese invasion force had been intercepted by American intelligence. There they conducted long-range reconnaissance missions, and between June 3 and 5, the Seventh Air Force B-17s flew sixteen attack missions involving fifty-five sorties, while a torpedo attack was flown by four USAAF B-26s. The Seventh Air Force planes scored twenty-two hits on enemy ships and downed ten fighters. The major combat actions at Midway were, however, conducted by U.S. Navy carrier-based aircraft.

In the Aleutians, a small number of B-17s and a larger number of B-24s would conduct occasional raids against Attu and Kiska from bases in Alaska over the ensuing months. Attu was finally recaptured by Allied troops in May 1943 and the Japanese abandoned Kiska two months later, prior to the Allied landings.

In the Southwest Pacific, Fifth Air Force B-17s targeted Lae on average once a week during June and the first week of July, and were launched against Rabaul twice a week. There, they bombed the port and warehouse areas, as well as troop concentrations and the

Vunakanau and Lakunai airfields. Other targets included Salamaua on the northeastern coast of New Guinea, Dili and Kupang on Timor Island, and Kendari on Celebes Island. Later in July, targets in New Guinea included shipping, landing barges, storage dumps, antiaircraft fire positions, and the Allied troop concentrations at Buna and Gona aimed at impeding the Japanese advance along the Kokoda trail.

On July 23, B-17s began photo reconnaissance missions over islands that were, or would be, the scene of important land battles. Seventh Air Force B-17s, staging through Canton Island, photographed Makin Island, while SOPAC B-17s of the 11th Bombardment Group (Heavy) on New Caledonia Island began photographing the Solomon Islands, specifically Guadalcanal, Tulagi, and Gavutu.

At the end of the month, the 11th began settling into its new base on Espiritu Santo Island, from which it would fly bombing and reconnaissance missions in support of upcoming U.S. Marine Corps operations in the Solomons. Between July 31 and August 7, these B-17s would fly fifty-six

An Eighth Air Force B-17 Flying Fortress assaults a railyard target (lower right) in German-occupied Europe. A canal crosses the frame diagonally. *USAAF via National Archives*

bombing missions and twenty-two reconnaissance sorties in support of the Guadalcanal operations.

During August and September, the Fifth Air Force B-17s targeted Rabaul on average once a week, and targets in New Guinea, especially Lae, about twice a week. Among the Rabaul missions was one on August 7 that involved thirteen Flying Fortresses of the 19th Bombardment Group (Heavy) that bombed Vunakanau Airfield to suppress Japanese offensive operations during the Marine Corps landings on Guadalcanal. Through most of the month, B-17s flew reconnaissance missions over the Solomon Islands to observe any possible surprise against the forces consolidating the Guadalcanal beachhead.

On August 13 and 14, B-17s and B-26s intercepted and mauled a convoy headed toward Basabua, near Gona on New Guinea. On August 17 and 18, a single B-17 targeted Kavieng on New Ireland Island. Further antiship action came on August 24 during the Battle of the Eastern Solomons, as seven B-17s and bombers from the carriers USS *Enterprise* and USS *Saratoga* blasted a Japanese task force covering transports bound for Guadalcanal. The following day, B-17s from Espiritu Santo sank the destroyer *Mutsuki*. On September 11, a Fifth Air Force Flying Fortress decimated the destroyer *Yayoi* off New Guinea.

The ability of the Boeing B-17 to absorb tremendous battle damage and still return to base safely is clearly illustrated in this post-mission photo of an Eighth Air Force Flying Fortress. The picture also shows the terrible effect of the German 88mm flak guns. A split second later, or a foot closer, and this Fort would never have made it. *USAAF via National Archives*

At a base in North Africa, USAAF ground crewmen pick though the remnants of a B-17 Flying Fortress—possibly attached to the Twelfth Air Force—that survived a rough landing only to have the fuselage burst into flames. *USAAF via National Archives*

Later in September, Fifth Air Force B-17s flew numerous missions against Japanese coastal shipping and troop concentrations around New Guinea in support of Allied troops on the ground. On September 17, Japanese ground forces were forced to halt their offensive within sight of Port Moresby because of a lack of reinforcements and supplies. Throughout the month and into October, B-17s and other bombers struck targets around Buna and Gona, as well as Menari, Kagi, Myola Lake, the Kokoda area, and Wairopi.

During October, Fifth Air Force Flying Fortress missions against the Japanese on Rabaul averaged two a week, but for the remainder of the year, such missions were much less frequent. The primary B-17 action through the end of 1942 would involve missions in support of the New Guinea ground operations.

On November 29, Fifth Air Force B-17s intercepted four destroyers carrying troops from Rabaul to Gona through the Vitiaz Strait between New Britain and New Guinea, damaging two and forcing the others to withdraw. On December 2, B-17s would be part of a strike on four destroyers off Gona, forcing the ships to offload the troops they carried in the wrong place. On December 8, B-17s succeeded in preventing another six destroyers from landing troops to reinforce the Buna-Gona beachhead.

While the Flying Fortresses continued to serve the Fifth Air Force in a combat role, commanders in the SOPAC area—the future Thirteenth Air Force domain—found the aircraft most useful in a reconnaissance role. This was illustrated on October 11, when B-17s observed and tracked a Japanese task force of cruisers and destroyers en route to Guadalcanal Island. The result was a U.S. Navy victory in the Battle of Cape Esperance.

A month later, on November 12, SOPAC B-17s shadowed a Japanese task force of eleven transports carrying thirteen thousand five hundred troops and escorted by cruisers and the battleships *Kirishima* and *Hiei* as they traveled toward Guadalcanal Island. One B-17 sighted a carrier 350 miles off Guadalcanal and followed the ship despite efforts by the Japanese to shoot it down. In the process, the Flying Fortress crew shot down a half dozen Mitsubishi A6M "Zero" fighters. Thanks to B-17s, the U.S. Navy would win another important surface action against the Imperial Japanese Navy.

Despite the demonstration of their value as reconnaissance aircraft within the theater, B-17s continued strike missions within the SOPAC in October and thereafter, targeting the Shortland Islands, as well as Buka and Bougainville in the Solomon Islands. During December, B-17s flew twenty-one strikes against Munda on New Georgia Island in the Solomons, as the Japanese desperately attempted to build airfields in the area.

Between December 18 and 26, Fifth Air Force B-17s bombed a Japanese convoy in Astrolabe Bay off Madang, and other shipping near Finschhafen and Cape Ward Hunt on the northern coast of New Guinea. Concluding the year, B-17s flew three missions against Rabaul between Christmas and December 30.

THE EUROPEAN THEATER OF OPERATIONS

At the Arcadia conference, Churchill and Roosevelt agreed on a policy of defeating Germany before Japan, and the USAAF offensive role in that activity would be to pull together a heavy bomber force to wage strategic warfare against the Third Reich. That force would have to be built from scratch as soon as possible. The first tangible step came on February 20, 1942, as Brigadier

General Ira Eaker arrived in the United Kingdom with six staff officers to set up shop as the Army Air Forces in Britain (AAFIB). Meanwhile, the VIII Bomber Command was created on January 19 and was incorporated into the Eighth Air Force, which was created fifteen days later. By the end of February, the VIII Bomber Command was under Eaker's leadership.

The Yanks studied the Royal Air Force (RAF) Bomber Command operations and worked with them to plan a cooperative air offensive. Joint operational committees dealing with targets, reconnaissance, and operations were set up in July. Over the following few weeks, a strategy would evolve under which the RAF would continue carpet-bombing German targets by night, while the USAAF would undertake a policy of conducting precision bombing missions in daylight.

On April 12, 1942, USAAF Commanding General Henry H. "Hap" Arnold formalized plans for the establishment of the Eighth Air Force in the United Kingdom as the USAAF component in the strategic war against Germany. On May 2, Major General Carl Spaatz was named as the Eighth Air Force commander. The Eighth Air Force would contain the VIII Bomber Command with heavy bombers, the VIII Interceptor Command (later Fighter Command), and the VIII Air Force Services Command. On June 20, General Dwight Eisenhower announced plans to integrate all of the American air units in the United Kingdom into the Eighth Air Force. In December, Eaker would replace Spaatz, as the latter was transferred to Algeria to serve as air adviser to General Eisenhower while major ground combat operations increased in the Mediterranean Theater.

A B-17F Flying Fortress in flight over a heavily forested mountainside, probably on a delivery flight. *USAAF via National Archives*

B-17s in 1942 with USAAF markings blast enemy facilities at a port city on a European coastal estuary. *USAAF via National Archives*

Two B-17Es head inland for a strike against an enemy target in German-occupied Europe. In 1942, the bomber forces that were dispatched on strikes often numbered two dozen or fewer on any given day. *USAAF via National Archives*

A string of standard 500-pound high-explosive bombs plummets earthward from the bomb bay of a USAAF Flying Fortress. Note the flak explosions on the right. The German gunners had fused their shells to explode at various altitudes, apparently unsure where the American bombers were flying. *USAAF via National Archives*

By the end of May, Eighth Air Force personnel had started to arrive. The first B-17s of the 97th Bombardment Group (Heavy) arrived in England early in July, but they would not see action for more than a month. The debut USAAF air operation over Western Europe was conducted on the Fourth of July by American air crews flying American-built Douglas Bostons borrowed from the RAF.

Once it got under way, however, the Eighth Air Force buildup would go quickly. By mid-September 1942, the 91st, 92nd, 303rd, 304th, and 305th Bombardment Groups (Heavy) would be operational in England, each with three squadrons operating B-17Fs. Indeed, the Eighth Air Force was seen as so robust that it was asked to divert resources to aid in creating the Twelfth Air Force, earmarked for the Mediterranean Theater. Both the 97th and 301st Bombardment Groups (Heavy) were diverted from the Eighth to the Twelfth. The Eighth would continue to serve as a big brother to the Twelfth until the decisions made at the Casablanca Conference in January 1943 relieved it of that responsibility.

The Eighth Air Force's historic first mission of the war using B-17s was flown on August 17. A dozen Flying Fortresses struck the marshaling yard at Rouen/Sotteville in German-occupied France at 5:39 p.m. local time, beginning what would be the most intensive strategic bombing campaign in history and the one involving more aircraft than any other. Most of these would be B-17s. As for Rouen, its position as the crossroads of the

rail network in northern France would make it a repeated Eighth Air Force target over the years.

The second mission of the Eighth Air Force came three days later, on the morning of August 19. In this operation, twenty-four B-17s were launched and twenty reached the targets, which were the Luftwaffe fighter bases near Abbeville in northern France, home of the legendary Jagdstaffel (Fighter Squadron) 26. An additional half-dozen Flying Fortresses flew a diversion. The objective was to engage the Luftwaffe so as to prevent them from intervening against the Allied commando operation at the French port city of Dieppe. In this mission, three B-17s were damaged.

The third B-17 mission in the European Theater came the next day, as eleven bombers struck the Amiens marshaling yard in France. On August 21, a dozen B-17s were sent to the shipyards at Rotterdam, Netherlands, but the mission was aborted when they were intercepted by twenty-five Bf.109s and Fw.190s. The USAAF reported two Luftwaffe aircraft shot down and one bomber damaged.

On August 24, in the fifth mission of the Eighth Air Force, a dozen B-17s struck the shipyard of Ateliers et Chantiers Maritime de la Seine at Le Trait in France. This time, three B-17s were damaged. On August 27, seven B-17s completed the mission against the shipyards at Rotterdam, and the next day, eleven B-17s struck the Potez aircraft factory at Méaulte in France. August 29 saw eleven B-17s bomb the Luftwaffe base at Courtrai in northern France. The Eighth Air Force and its precision

B-17Fs cannibalized for parts in North Africa—*Little Eva* had surrendered her guns, tires, Hamilton Standard propellers, and even her wingtips. *USAAF via National Archives*

bombing procedure were still on the learning curve, and the lessons would soon become more intense.

Using a significantly larger armada than previously launched, the Eighth Air Force sent thirty-seven B-17s over France on September 5. Of these, thirty-one succeeded in bombing the Rouen/Sotteville marshaling yard. The next day, the Eighth Air Force sent seventy-six bombers over France. Of these, thirty B-17s struck the Potez plant and eleven bombed Luftwaffe bases near Saint-Omer. While B-17s had been damaged by interceptors on earlier missions, this time two were shot down.

On September 7, the B-17s headed for targets in the Netherlands, but the weather was so poor that most aborted. Four B-17s attempted to hit the Wilton shipyards at Rotterdam, and five sought targets of opportunity around Utrecht. Weather hampered operations through September, but on October 2, thirty-eight B-17s flew a repeat of the September 6 mission without a loss. On October 9, fifty-nine B-17s struck factories in the French industrial city of Lille, while others attacked Luftwaffe bases at Longuenesse and Roubaix.

In October, against the backdrop of the heavy losses to Allied shipping from the activities of the German U-boat wolf packs, the highest command levels of the USAAF ordered the Eighth to address the problem. The U-boat pens, mainly located on the French western coast, were added to the Eighth Air Force target lists, and tactics for attacking these heavily fortified facilities were developed.

A recently repaired Twelfth Air Force B-17 Flying Fortress is cleaned at a secret aircraft repair facility prior to returning to action. Located 1,400 miles south of the Mediterranean Theater front lines, in the Eritrea region of Ethiopia, this operation was known simply as "Project 19." During the summer of 1941, the German army had advanced far enough on the North African front to present a serious threat to the Suez Canal. Though America was not yet in the war, the Roosevelt Administration agreed to a clandestine effort to aid the British in protecting the canal from falling under Axis control. Project 19 was one aspect of this. On November 19, 1941, two weeks before the United States entered the war, the Douglas Aircraft Company was assigned the task of managing the facility and recruiting the staff. *Courtesy Harry Gann*

October 20 saw a mission against the pens at Lorient, but most of the sixty-six B-17s were frustrated by cloud cover. Another eight B-17s bombed the Cherbourg Luftwaffe base. On November 7, fifty-six B-17s and eleven B-24s struck the U-boat pens at Brest, and two days later, thirty-one B-17s and a dozen B-24s struck the U-boat base at Saint-Nazaire. On November 14, fifteen B-17s and nine B-24s returned to Saint-Nazaire when the pens at La Pallice were obscured by clouds. Between November 17 and 23, the Eighth Air Force sent heavy bombers to Saint-Nazaire three times, also targeting Lorient twice and La Pallice once. By the end of the month, the B-17s had disrupted U-boat operations, but the U-boat pens themselves were too heavily fortified to have sustained major damage.

Weather had precluded many other missions that year, but on November 8, eleven B-17s struck an Abbeville Luftwaffe base and thirty-one bombed a locomotive factory at Lille. Nearly a month later, on December 6, those two targets would be revisited by B-17s. On December 12, the target was the heavily defended marshaling yard at Rouen. On December 20, the target for seventy-two Eighth Air Force bombers was the Luftwaffe arsenal at Romilly.

The last mission of the year, attacked by forty bombers on December 30, was again the U-boat base at Lorient. There were three B-17s lost to Luftwaffe interceptors on that year's final mission.

The B-17s and the Eighth Air Force evolved greatly in the European Theater during 1942. The Flying Fortress had more than gotten its baptism of fire, and it was beginning to prove itself as a potent weapon that could take it and dish it out. From nothing, the Eighth Air Force had built a sizable force in very little time. Its VIII Bomber Command had become the largest bomber force in American history, but that was a mere sliver of what it would become in the following year.

THE MEDITERRANEAN THEATER OF OPERATIONS

While USAAF strategic operations from bases in England were organized under a very methodical plan, their counterparts in the Mediterranean Theater were cobbled together almost haphazardly. Indeed, the first major USAAF strategic mission in the theater was flown in the chaotic early days of the war before there even was an organization.

Flown on June 12, 1942, this first mission involved B-24s. In May 1942, Colonel Harry A. Halverson was

The secret Project 19 in Eritrea, staffed by Americans and locally recruited crews, began servicing both USAAF and Royal Air Force aircraft in 1942. The project did heavy repair and modification work that was not possible at British bases in Egypt, including propeller repair. Project 19 even designed and manufactured such gear as auxiliary fuel tanks. The facility is credited with helping the British win the pivotal Battle of El Alamein in October 1942. Project 19 was terminated late in 1943, and the base was dismantled. *Courtesy Harry Gann*

ordered to take twenty-three Liberators straight from the factory to bases in China and launch a raid against Tokyo. This mission, known as the Halverson Project (HALPRO), proceeded across the Atlantic and across North Africa. In Egypt, Halverson was handed a change of plans. The new mission was to attack Ploesti, Romania, home of the enormous oil refining and storage complex that accounted for about a third of German petroleum supplies. As with the Doolittle raid on Tokyo two months earlier, Halverson's attack came as a stunning surprise to the enemy but did little actual damage. Ploesti would continue to be a key target for B-17s and B-24s for the rest of the war.

The organization for the USAAF strategic campaign reached the Mediterranean on June 28, 1942, when Major General Lewis Brereton arrived in Cairo from his previous command with the Tenth Air Force in India. His task was to establish the U.S. Army Middle East Air Forces (USAMEAF), a new organization consisting of Halverson's B-24s and a handful of aircraft that Brereton had brought with him from India. Among them were the B-17Es of the 9th Bombardment Squadron (Heavy) that arrived in Lydda, Palestine, from Allahabad, India, the next day.

A B-17 Flying Fortress is framed against a display of what appears to be friendly antiaircraft fire. It may also be celebratory fireworks. During 1942, Allied bomber bases, especially in North Africa and the Pacific, were often attacked by enemy aircraft. Within a year, however, the Allies had achieved air supremacy over their own bases. *USAAF via National Archives*

The first USAMEAF mission, flown on the night of July 2, involved B-17s and B-24s bombing the harbor at German-occupied Tobruk, Libya. B-17s returned to this target seven times between July 8 and the end of the month.

In August, Brereton outlined the objectives for USAAF assets in the Mediterranean Theater, which included destroying the German Afrika Korps, achieving air superiority over the Mediterranean, and undertaking strategic operations against Italy and other targets, including Ploesti. For the ensuing year, the USAAF would closely integrate its operations with those of the British Royal Air Force in that theater.

In October, after a long period of building up squadron strength with new aircraft arriving from the United States, USAMEAF B-17s were once again in action, with two missions against Tobruk and an October 20 strike on a coastal road near Bardia after a mission against Tobruk was scrubbed because of cloud cover.

November marked major changes in the Mediterranean Theater, beginning on the eighth with Operation Torch, which involved simultaneous Allied landings in Morocco and Algeria. The pro-German Vichy French forces in control of the region quickly switched sides as thirty-five thousand American troops landed. Meanwhile, the British

Eighth Army had defeated the Afrika Korps at El Alamein on November 5 and had gained the initiative in Northeast Africa. The Germans found themselves being squeezed from both sides.

With the strategic situation now greatly changed, the USAAF assets in the theater would be reorganized on November 12 and 13. Brereton's short-lived USAMEAF was replaced by the Ninth Air Force and given the responsibility for Northeast Africa and the eastern Mediterranean. Meanwhile, the Twelfth Air Force, previously organized in England and supported by the Eighth Air Force, moved south to take up responsibility for USAAF operations in Northwest Africa and the western Mediterranean.

Early in November, B-17s conducted missions against Tobruk and against the harbor at Candia on Crete, and on November 14 and 18, Ninth Air Force Flying Fortresses targeted the harbor at Benghazi, Libya, through which Afrika Korps supplies flowed. On November 27, they bombed shipping at Portolago Bay in the Dodecanese Islands.

Twelfth Air Force B-17s got into action on November 16 as six B-17s of the 97th Bombardment Group (Heavy), based at Maison Blanche, Algeria, attacked Sidi Ahmed Airfield at Bizerte in Tunisia. That same group had flown the first B-17 mission over Europe on August 17. On November 20, it was turnabout time as the Luftwaffe began a series of counterraids on the Twelfth Air Force B-17 base at Maison Blanche, compelling temporary relocation of the B-17s to Tafaraoui.

Twelfth Air Force B-17s bombed the Luftwaffe bases at El Aouina in Tunisia five times between November 19 and December 15, and bombed targets at the big port city of Bizerte a dozen times between November 28 and December 31. The Bizerte targets included the harbor, airfields, railyards, and bridges. During December, B-17s also targeted troop concentrations, mainly in the Gabes and Sfax areas, and in Tunis four times between December 5 and December 31, as well as harbor installations at Sousse several times in the last few days of 1942.

There were tremendous gains for the Allies in the Mediterranean Theater during 1942. The following year would see an end to the Axis presence in Africa and a beginning to Allied operations in Italy. The growing number of B-17s in the theater would have plenty of work to do.

A field modification gave this Fifth Air Force B-17E additional forward armament to deal with frontal attacks by Japanese A6M Zero fighters. In 1943, *The Last Straw* was operational in the Southwest Pacific with the New Guinea–based 63rd Bombardment Squadron of the 43rd Bombardment Group. *USAAF via National Archives*

The B-17F Flying Fortress *Aztec's Curse* over Guadalcanal on a low-level attack on Japanese positions. While large bomber formations were common over European targets, it was typical in the Pacific Theater for Flying Fortresses to fly missions alone or in groups of a half dozen or fewer. This bomber was operational with both the 26th Bombardment Squadron of the 11th Bombardment Group and with the 31st Bombardment Squadron of the 5th Bombardment Group. *USAAF via National Archives*

CHAPTER FOUR

B-17 OPERATIONS IN 1943

THE PACIFIC THEATER OF OPERATIONS

As 1943 began, Flying Fortress activities continued in two of the three areas within the Pacific Theater. In the Southwest Pacific, the Fifth Air Force, commanded by General George Kenney, continued operations in New Guinea and neighboring New Britain. In the South Pacific area, the focus of the action was in the Solomon Islands. It was there that USAAF assets would be placed under the command of the Thirteenth Air Force, nicknamed "Jungle Air Force," which was created in January 1943 under the command of General Nathan Twining. The headquarters of the Thirteenth Air Force were transferred from Noumea in New Caledonia to Espiritu Santo Island in the New Hebrides on January 20.

The Seventh Air Force in the Central Pacific, meanwhile, had already adopted the B-24, rather than the B-17, as its standard heavy bomber. Throughout 1943, the number of B-24s in all of the Pacific areas would increase as the number of B-17s declined through attrition. By year's end, the B-24 was the standard heavy bomber across the Pacific. During 1943, the USAAF made the decision to terminate deliveries of replacement

B-17s to the Pacific and to concentrate its existing and future B-17 force against Germany.

Also in 1943, in the Southwest Pacific, the Fifth Air Force came to rely less on heavy bombers and more on lighter aircraft. Because distances were relatively short, the Fifth Air Force operated with larger and larger numbers of A-20 light bombers and B-25 medium bombers. In the actions in and around New Guinea, these two types came to be the most commonly deployed Allied bombers.

On New Year's Day, B-17s and B-24s targeted the airfields at Rabaul, New Britain Island, and Gasmata Island in the Bismarck Archipelago, and Lae, New Guinea. A continuation of the mission profiles flown late in 1942, these operations would set the pattern for the new year. During January and February, Fifth Air Force B-17s would average at least two strikes on Rabaul each week, while continuing their missions against Japanese shipping around New Guinea. On the January 5 Rabaul mission, one of two B-17s shot down cost the life of Brigadier General Kenneth Walker, the commander of the Fifth Air Forces V Bomber Command.

Also on January 5, B-17s bombed a Japanese cruiser near Bougainville in the Solomon Islands. Additional missions

A Boeing B-17F, seen from the bombardier's position in a B-17E, releases its ordnance on an enemy target. The United States insignia on this bomber was introduced in June 1943 and was superseded two months later. Before, the standard American national insignia was a white star in a solid dark blue circle. In June 1943, two white rectangles were added at the sides, and the whole insignia had a red perimeter. In August, the order went out to change the red outline to dark blue, but in the field, many of the red outlines were not repainted until much later. *USAAF via National Archives*

against Bougainville were flown by Jungle Air Force B-17s throughout the month. During the middle of the month, B-17s were called into service to airlift rations, water, and ammunition from Henderson Field on Guadalcanal to front-line troops. By February 9, the hard-fought battle for Guadalcanal officially ended with the bloody island finally under American control.

On January 19 and 20, Thirteenth Air Force B-17s attacked the Japanese airfield at Munda on New Georgia Island, and on January 22, they targeted shipping in Rekata Bay on Santa Isabel Island.

In February, the Fifth Air Force Flying Fortresses bombed targets throughout the Bismarck Archipelago, including Rabaul, Gasmata Island, Simpson Harbor, the

Cape Gazelle area, the airfield at Cape Gloucester, Ubili, the Watom Islands, and shipping near Kokop and Cape Nelson. On February 19 and 20, they hit the seaplane base between Buin and Faisi, as well as Kahili Airfield, both on Bougainville.

March opened with the pivotal Battle of the Bismarck Sea, an important moment for the Fifth Air Force and a very bad one for Japan. Like the Battle of Midway, this battle was characterized by the defeat of a Japanese naval force entirely by Allied air power.

On February 28, the Japanese made an effort to reinforce their New Guinea forces by sending in the 51st Division aboard a flotilla of eight destroyers and eight troop ships bound from Rabaul. On March 3, nearly 100

First Lieutenant Bascom Smith, a young pilot based in England, smiles from the window of his Eighth Air Force bomber. *USAAF via National Archives*

Royal Australian Air Force and USAAF Fifth Air Force bombers, including twenty-eight B-17s of the 43rd Bombardment Group (Heavy), struck the Japanese ships near Cape Ward Hunt. By midafternoon, all the transports and three destroyers were sunk, and a fourth went down by the end of the day. The remaining destroyers recovered the survivors, but only about 12 percent of the Japanese troops intended to reinforce the New Guinea garrison actually made it.

For the remainder of the month and through April, Fifth Air Force B-17s continued their actions against Japanese bases, such as Wewak on New Guinea, and shipping in the area around New Guinea. Fifth Air Force targets in the Bismarck Archipelago, including Ulamoa, Finschhafen, and the airfield at Kavieng, were attacked during April, often by lone B-17s.

By that time, as the base at Rabaul became more difficult to supply, its value to the Japanese diminished. As that occurred, Rabaul gradually ceased to be a threat to Allied forces, and Fifth Air Force bombing raids against it tapered off. Eventually, the Japanese abandoned their garrison on New Britain, leaving those still there to fend for themselves without resupply. Allied forces simply bypassed the island rather than invading it.

Later in March and into April, Thirteenth Air Force B-17s, often operating singly, bombed targets such as Munda Airfield on New Georgia, Vila Airfield on Kolombangara, Gasmata Island, Cape Gloucester, Kahili, and Ballale.

From May through July, there were few large-scale operations involving heavy bombers in the Pacific Theater. An exception was the fifty-plane raid by a mixed force of B-17s and B-24s against airfields in the Rabaul area on June 10. It was one of just a handful of attacks conducted against Rabaul during that period. Many B-17 actions involved just a single aircraft, and most involved small numbers. The raids were mainly focused against airfields and coastal targets, especially barges and light shipping, in or near New Guinea and the Solomons. Often, the missions were flown at night.

The next major air assault came on July 25, when the Thirteenth Air Force launched the heaviest attack yet seen in the South Pacific. The strike package involved more than one hundred seventy bombers, including USAAF B-17s, B-24s, and B-25s, as well as navy Grumman Avenger torpedo bombers (TBFs) and Douglas Dauntless scout bombers (SBDs), supported by more than seventy fighters. They dropped more than 145 tons of bombs in about thirty minutes in support of the final assault to capture Munda. That record air attack was topped three weeks later in the August 13 attack by the Fifth Air Force at Salamaua, New Guinea. A total of fifty-nine B-17s, B-24s, and B-26s dropped 175 tons of bombs during the attack.

Other notable Fifth Air Force B-17 actions during August included a sweep across New Guinea on August 3 in the company of B-25s and B-24s that targeted aircraft, watercraft, trails, and military camps in and around areas such as Bogadjim, Salamaua, Manokwari, and Larat, and along the Bubui, Masaweng, Mindjim, and Kofebi Rivers and Bogadjim Road. A similar sweep six days later saw strikes at Salamaua, Lae, Nuk Nuk, bridges on the Bogadjim-Ramu Road, positions along Borgen Bay on New Britain Island, and installations at Unea Island in the Bismarck Archipelago, as well as targets of opportunity at Alilit and Amboina Island in the Moluccas.

On August 25, in a follow-up to the August 13 attack, the Fifth Air Force assembled almost 100 B-17s,

A Flying Fortress of the Eighth Air Force 381st Bombardment Group wings its way across the English Channel wearing standard USAAF insignia for the summer of 1943. *USAAF via National Archives*

B-24s, and B-25s for an hour-long assault against the Hansa Bay area, Nubia, and Awar in New Guinea.

During September, Fifth Air Force B-17s continued to operate with other bomber types against targets in New Guinea, but by then the Flying Fortresses were nearing the end of their service in the Pacific Theater. The USAAF had decided to make the B-24 the standard heavy bomber in the Pacific because it had a slightly longer range (depending on fuel and bomb load) than the B-17. On October 5, a small number of B-17s bombed the Bogadjim Road and jetties at Erima on New Guinea. Thereafter, the B-17 was no longer part of the USAAF roster for major operations in the Pacific.

THE EUROPEAN THEATER OF OPERATIONS

The third week of January 1943 was marked by a conference in Casablanca in which President Franklin Roosevelt and British Prime Minister Winston Churchill, together with their key military leaders, met to discuss global strategy. Among other key decisions, they agreed that they would accept nothing short of unconditional surrender from the Axis powers. As for strategic air operations against Germany, they confirmed earlier understandings that the Eighth Air Force and the RAF Bomber Command would share the primary objective of destroying the German military, economic, and industrial complex, as well as the morale of the German people. The joint operation, which had been informally ongoing since mid-1942, would be formalized as the Combined Bomber Offensive (CBO). The CBO officially began in May 1943, when the Eighth Air Force got enough heavy bombers into the theater to make it theoretically possible to launch 100 or more every day.

The famous Casablanca directive stated that the primary objective of the strategic air campaign was "the progressive destruction and dislocation of the German military, industrial, and economic system, and the undermining of the morale of the German people to a point where their capacity for armed resistance was fatally weakened."

The directive named five primary target systems in the following order of priority: German U-boat construction yards, German aircraft industry, the transportation network within Germany and occupied Europe, the German oil industry, and other industrial targets related to war production.

That selection, wide enough in itself, was further qualified by the statement that "the above order of priority may be varied from time to time according to developments in the strategic situation. Other objectives of great importance either from the political or economic point of view must be attacked."

It was clear from that statement that the Casablanca Conference intended to give maximum freedom to the commanders of the air forces to act according to their own judgment. That also explains the absence of a definitive statement on such vital issues as the choice between general and specific target systems, or the alternative strategies of destruction of morale by area bombing (favored by the British) versus attacking specific economic targets with precision bombing (favored by the USAAF).

Tactically, 1943 would see the Eighth Air Force obtain better precision bombing results as it switched from individual targeting to bomber attacks in formation, seen as a better way to defend against enemy interceptors. When weather prevented formations to launch as a group, the pilots took off singly using instruments and formed up while airborne using radio beacons.

Eighth Air Force operations for the new year got under way on January 3 with sixty B-17s and eight B-24s dropping 171 tons of bombs on the U-boat pens at Saint-Nazaire. U-boat facilities at Brest and Lorient would be hit on January 23, and the U-boat yard at Emden in Germany would be a target of opportunity on January 27 and February 1. These were the first raids against the U-boat facilities since the big effort in November 1942. In the meantime, sixty-four B-17s bombed factories and railyards at Lille on January 13.

The mission on January 27 marked the first attack by the Eighth Air Force on targets within Germany. The primary target, the naval yard at Wilhelmshaven, was hit by fifty-three B-17s and two others diverted to Emden. Back in July 1941, when only the RAF operated Flying Fortresses, Wilhelmshaven had been the first-ever strategic target attacked by a member of the Boeing 299 family.

An armada of B-17Fs from the Framlingham-based 390th Bombardment Group encounters light flak over a German Luftwaffe air field near Amiens in northern France's Picardy region. *USAAF via National Archives*

In a tragic accident over Berlin, bombs from one 94th Bombardment Group Flying Fortress lop off part of the tail of another bomber. No parachutes were seen before the stricken Fort dropped into the clouds below. *USAAF via National Archives*

On February 2, an attempted second attack on Germany was aborted because of weather. Two days later, and again on February 14, B-17s struck the marshaling yard and factories around Emden. There were thirty-nine Flying Fortresses in the first raid and seventy-four in the second. On February 16 and 27, U-boat facilities were again on the target list. On the first date, fifty-nine B-17s and six B-24s hit Saint-Nazaire, and on the latter date, forty-six B-17s and fourteen B-24s dropped 155 tons of bombs at Brest. Six B-17s and two B-24s went down in the first raid, but damage was minimal at Brest. Other naval targets also figured in the target list that month as fifty-nine B-17s struck Wilhelmshaven on February 26.

During March, Wilhelmshaven was attacked again on the 22nd by sixty-nine B-17s, with U-boat facilities on the target list, while Lorient was revisited by sixty-five B-17s that hit the power plant, bridge, and port area. Another port attack against Germany would occur on March 18, as seventy-three Flying Fortresses bombed Vegesack, near Bremen. Meanwhile, the port at Rotterdam was targeted by twenty-eight B-17s on March 4 and thirty-three B-17s on March 13. Hamm, in the industrial Ruhr area of Germany, was visited by sixteen B-17s on March 4.

March would also see a major effort against rail targets in northern France. Rouen was attacked three times between March 8 and 28 with an average of sixty-two B-17s, and Amiens was hit on March 13 by seventy-five Flying Fortresses.

In April, operations began on the fourth with eighty-five B-17s dropping 251 tons of bombs on factories in the Paris area, especially that of the Renault vehicle company. The next day, eighty-two B-17s dropped 245.5 tons of bombs on industrial sites in the Belgian port of Antwerp. That city would be targeted again on May 4 by sixty-five B-17s. On April 17, the Eighth Air Force launched a major assault involving 115 B-17s against Bremen, specifically targeting the Focke Wulf aircraft plant. Luftwaffe opposition was especially fierce, and fifteen Flying Fortresses were shot down by interceptors.

Several major assaults on U-boat facilities would come during April and May. On April 16, fifty-nine B-17s bombed the base at Lorient, while sixteen B-24s hit Brest. On May 1, despite bad weather that stymied most of the strike package and vicious Luftwaffe opposition, twenty-nine B-17s hit Saint-Nazaire.

During the second week of May, the arrival in England of the 94th, 95th, and 96th Bombardment Groups (Heavy), each with four squadrons of B-17Fs, greatly enhanced the Eighth Air Force's ability to get large numbers of aircraft over the target. It would mark the point from which hundred-plane raids would become routine.

On May 13, the new units participated in attacks against targets in northern France, including the Potez plant at Mééaulte and Luftwaffe bases around Saint-Omer. The former was attacked by eighty-eight B-17s, and the latter was struck by thirty-one Flying Fortresses. Total losses numbered four bombers.

During the two weeks beginning on May 14, the newly expanded Eighth Air Force launched a series of very large raids, mainly into Germany, with U-boat yards and port facilities high on the target list. On the first day, 126 B-17s and seventeen B-24s hit Kiel, while thirty-eight B-17s bombed Antwerp and thirty-four B-17s bombed the Luftwaffe base at Courtrai. The main targets in Antwerp were vehicle factories that had, ironically, been previously owned by American automakers Ford and General Motors.

The next day, seventy-six B-17s bombed Helgoland and Wilhelmshaven, while another fifty-nine struck at Emden. On May 17, 118 B-17s hit Lorient, and another thirty-nine bombed the port at Bordeaux in France. Two days later, 103 B-17s returned to Kiel, and sixty-four bombed the port of Flensburg. On May 21, Wilhelmshaven received another visit from seventy-seven Flying Fortresses, while sixty-three bombers hit Emden again. On May 29, the Eighth Air Force ended the month with 147 B-17s targeting the U-boat pens at Saint-Nazaire and fifty-seven hitting the naval base at Rennes.

Among the B-17s flying the May 17 mission against Lorient was the first Eighth Air Force heavy bomber crew to complete its full quota of twenty-five missions and hence to be qualified to return home. The aircraft was the famous B-17F commanded by Captain Robert Morgan and nicknamed *Memphis Belle*. Assigned to the 324th Bombardment Squadron of the 91st Bombardment Group, the aircraft had been the subject of William Wyler's USAAF documentary film entitled *Memphis Belle: A Story of a Flying Fortress*. Back in the United States, the film, the plane, and the crew would participate in war bond tours.

During June, only two missions continued the ongoing campaign against the U-boats before the Eighth Air Force turned to other strategic targets. On June 11, 218 B-17s bombed Wilhelmshaven and Cuxhaven. Two days

This B-17F Flying Fortress, with standard insignia for early 1943, was assigned to the 91st Bombardment Group of the Eighth Air Force. In March 1943, as the aircraft and crew were deployed overseas, they stopped at the Brookley Field repair center near Mobile, Alabama, to have the engines replaced because of inadvertently inverted piston rings. At the Battlehouse Hotel bar in downtown Mobile, pilot First Lieutenant Loren Roll met Mary Ruth King, a sheetmetal worker from the Brookley Field facility. A week later they were married, and he named the airplane *Mary Ruth, Memories of Mobile*. In England, Roll and his crew were assigned to the 92nd Bombardment Group replacement pool, while *Mary Ruth, Memories of Mobile* was assigned to the 91st Group. She was shot down on June 22, 1943, but Roll flew thirty-one missions and returned stateside to his bride. They lived in Montana, Roll's home state, and Washington before retiring to Alabama in 2000. Loren and Mary Ruth celebrated their sixtieth wedding anniversary in March 2003. *USAAF via National Archives*

later, 122 Flying Fortresses attacked Bremen and sixty bombed Kiel. The Luftwaffe interceptors put up one of their best defenses yet, and more than twenty-four B-17s were shot down.

In June 1943, the CBO issued a narrower targeting directive, establishing the Operation Pointblank target system. The Combined Chiefs of Staff ordered the Eighth Air Force to attack Germany's fighter interceptor strength as the top priority objective, targeting airframe, engine, and component factories, as well as aircraft repair and storage depots, and enemy interceptors in the air and on the ground. Under Pointblank, U-boat yards and bases were defined as secondary objectives. After the victories in the North Atlantic in May 1943, it was clear that detecting and sinking U-boats at sea was far more effective than bombing the heavily reinforced concrete of the yards and submarine pens. U-boats ceased thereafter to be priority targets for the strategic bombing campaign, although the targets were not abandoned entirely.

On June 22, the Eighth Air Force conducted a massive raid on the Ruhr industrial area in which 183 B-17s took out a major synthetic rubber factory, while thirty-nine

other B-17s blasted the vehicle plants at Antwerp. Three days later, the Eighth Air Force sent 275 B-17s against Bremen and Hamburg, but they diverted on account of cloud cover and only 167 hit targets of opportunity. On June 26, fifty-seven Flying Fortresses bombed Luftwaffe bases and depots in northern France.

June 28 saw another attack on U-boat facilities as 158 B-17s attacked Saint-Nazaire. On the same day, another forty-three Flying Fortresses hit the Beaumont-le-Roger Luftwaffe base. An attempt to attack Luftwaffe targets in France again the following day had to abort because of weather, but seventy-six other B-17s managed to strike the aircraft engine factory at Le Mans.

On the Fourth of July, the Eighth Air Force went back to Le Mans, targeting factories both there and in Nantes with 166 Flying Fortresses. Meanwhile, another seventy-one B-17s bombed the U-boat base at La Pallice. On July 14, Bastille Day was marked by three Flying Fortress attacks in France. A factory at Villacoublay was hit by 101, while the Luftwaffe base at Amiens received the wrath of fifty-three B-17s, and another fifty-two bombed Le Bourget Luftwaffe base outside Paris.

Three days later, cloud cover over Germany spared most targets, although thirty-three bombers hit targets of opportunity and twenty-one B-17s tried and missed in an attempt to bomb the Fokker factory at Amsterdam.

On July 24, the Eighth Air Force B-17s undertook their first attacks against targets in Norway. These nineteen-hundred-mile missions were also the longest flown by the Eighth at that time. Factories at Heroya were hit by 167 bombers, while 41 bombers targeted the port of Trondheim. A mission against Bergen was aborted because of weather.

That night, the RAF launched a massive raid against Hamburg, and the Eighth Air Force followed with a 100-plane B-17 strike on the city on July 25, which began a sustained air campaign against targets in northern Germany that would be carried out by the Allies through the end of the month. The next day, ninety-six B-17s hit rubber factories in Hannover, fifty-four revisited Hamburg, and forty-nine bombed other targets. On July 28, aircraft plants were the target as fifty-eight B-17s bombed Kassel and thirty-seven hit Oschersleben. July 29 saw ninety-one B-17s strike the port of Kiel and fifty-four bomb the Heinkel factory in Warnemunde. On July 30, 134 Flying Fortresses concentrated on Feisler aircraft factories around Kassel.

In the latter half of August, the Eighth Air Force resumed the offensive against industrial targets in the Ruhr. On August 12, 243 Flying Fortresses attacked synthetic oil plants at Bochum, Gelsenkirchen, and Recklinghausen, and factories in Bonn.

On August 15 and 16, the Eighth Air Force began a major new offensive against its own major antagonist—the Luftwaffe. Over the ensuing weeks, numerous attacks would target the interceptor bases that so imperiled operations against Germany. During those two opening days, an average of 263 B-17s each day bombed air bases at Vlissingen in the Netherlands and in France at Abbeville, Amiens, Lille, and Poix, as well as the Luftwaffe depot at Le Bourget. Interceptors operating from these bases routinely hammered bomber formations before they had reached Germany.

An interim report issued on July 22 observed that one of the principal effects of the CBO was to put the Luftwaffe on the defensive. By that time, an estimated one-half of Germany's fighter strength was devoted to "defense of the Reich" missions. That was good news on the eastern and Mediterranean fronts, but not so good for the B-17 crews that faced hundreds of interceptors every day.

Technical Sergeant "Mexico" Barrazas in his station as a waist gunner aboard an Eighth Air Force B-17 Flying Fortress. *USAAF via National Archives*

The main consideration for the CBO under Operation Pointblank was the increasing strength of Germany's fighter defenses, which meant that strategic bombing should establish Allied air supremacy as a primary goal. The desire was to concentrate on targets that would affect front-line Luftwaffe strength fairly quickly. This was especially important because intelligence reports indicated ambitious plans to bolster the Luftwaffe. In the middle of 1943, the CBO chiefs feared that, unless prompt preventive measures were taken, new improved fighters—notably Focke Wulf Fw.190s—capable of devastating attacks against heavy bombers, would soon come off the production lines in huge numbers and shatter Allied hopes for air superiority.

Because the Eighth Air Force didn't have enough bombers to conduct a comprehensive campaign against the German aircraft industry, the leaders decided to zero in on the ball bearing industry. Ball bearings are an Achilles' heel of industry because they are required for all machinery. From a target-planning perspective, ball bearings were a brilliant choice because the German ball bearing industry was known to be concentrated in three cities, with the glittering prize of half the industry's total capacity located at Schweinfurt. However, the city was deeper inside Germany than Eighth Air Force bombers had conducted a major mission.

On August 17, the Eighth Air Force celebrated the first anniversary of its B-17 operations from England with 188 B-17s attacking Schweinfurt. Meanwhile, 127 Flying Fortresses bombed the Messerschmitt aircraft plant at Regensburg. It was a costly mission for German industry and for the Eighth Air Force as well. There were thirty-six B-17s lost in the Schweinfurt assault and twenty-four shot down on the Regensburg mission. It would be two months before the bombers returned to Schweinfurt.

On August 19 and 24, the Eighth Air Force resumed the campaign against the Luftwaffe bases, with 93 and 108 B-17s, respectively, hitting five targets. On August 31, 105 B-17s hit a Luftwaffe base near Amiens. Also on April 24, 85 B-17s that had flown to North Africa after the Regensburg raid attacked a Luftwaffe base near Bordeaux on their way back to England.

By that point, Allied photo reconnaissance aircraft had discovered that the Germans were constructing fixed launch facilities for V-1 cruise missiles and V-2 ballistic missiles in northern France. Those sites would be added to the Eighth Air Force's priority target list, and the first such mission was flown by 187 B-17s against the site at Watten on August 27. On September 7, 58 B-17s returned to the V-2 site at Watten. Most of the missions would involve V-1 missiles because they were launched primarily from the fixed sites. Most V-2s were launched from hard-to-locate mobile launchers. The air offensive against the missile sites, which would be ongoing until the Allies captured northern France a year later, were designated Operation Crossbow.

Although most missions scheduled for September 2 were scrubbed because of weather, the clouds cleared the next day and 196 B-17s hit five Luftwaffe facilities in France, and 37 bombed factories near Paris. On September 6, cloud cover hindered a large assault on German industry at Stuttgart, but 262 B-17s managed to hit mainly secondary targets. On September 7, 105 B-17s hit a Luftwaffe base near Brussels.

September 9 saw a maximum effort against targets in France that was designed to be a rehearsal for Eighth Air Force participation in the massive Allied land invasion of the continent that would take place the following spring, on June 6, 1944. In this maximum effort, the Eighth Air Force launched 330 B-17s and B-24s, the highest number to date. Of those, 68 B-17s hit targets in the

On May 17, 1943, the men of the *Memphis Belle*, a B-17F assigned to the 324th Bombardment Squadron of the 91st Bombardment Group, became the first Flying Fortress crew to complete twenty-five combat missions. Under Eighth Air Force rules, that made them eligible to end their fighting careers and return home to the United States. *USAAF via National Archives*

The famous nose art on the B-17F *Memphis Belle* was painted by 91st Bombardment Group artist Tony Starcer. The Fortress was named for Margaret Polk of Memphis, Tennessee, then the girlfriend of the aircraft's pilot, Lieutenant Robert Morgan. *USAAF via National Archives*

The *Memphis Belle* lands at Long Beach, California, during the summer of 1943. After the crew and its famous Flying Fortress completed twenty-five missions, the USAAF sent them stateside to tour the country as part of a war bond campaign. *Courtesy Harry Gann*

This view is from inside a Flying Fortress, looking down at the Sperry ball turret located just aft of the radio operator's station. In this contemporary photo, the twin gun belts are empty, but for combat operations each would have held 250 rounds of .50-caliber ammunition fed from twin boxes located adjacent to the turret hoist. Powered by an electric motor, the turret revolved 360 degrees and had a full field of fire beneath the Flying Fortress. *Bill Yenne*

This is the view from within the Sperry ball turret, looking aft through the bulletproof glass to the tail wheel resting on the tarmac. One of the two .50-caliber machine guns can be seen on the left, and the computing gun sight is in the center. The job of ball turret gunner was not for the faint of heart. Tall men, large men, and men touched with either claustrophobia or acrophobia need not have applied. Nor was there room for a parachute within the turret. The gunner entered the turret from within the aircraft, after which the turret was cranked down to its operational position. He then curled up in a fetal position, with his feet in stirrups and his knees by his ears, and waited for action. *Bill Yenne*

bombers returned on January 19 to bomb the industrial area south of Tunis and the marshaling yard at Jabal al Jallud. On January 5, B-17s struck the Sfax power station, and on January 11, B-17s hit the fort and town of Gadames, Libya, and the rail bridge and highway bridge across the Oued el Akarit, near Gabes, Tunisia.

On January 12, a dozen B-17s of the 97th Bombardment Group (Heavy) blasted the Castel Benito airfield south of Tripoli, Libya, dropping fragmentation clusters and one five-hundred-pound and six one-thousand-pound high-explosive bombs, destroying at least twenty parked aircraft. The base was hit again on January 18. On January 20, B-17s bombed Cap Mangin near Gabes, Tunisia, when cloud cover prevented bombing of the primary target at Tripoli. On January 22, B-17s operating in two waves struck El Aouina Luftwaffe base in Morocco in the morning, as B-26s bombed the airfield shortly after noon and B-25s attacked in the afternoon. Bizerte, an important target in late 1942, was bombed three times between January 23 and 31.

The first week of February saw Twelfth Air Force strikes on the harbor and shipping at Tunis and shipping in La Goulette harbor and the Gabes Luftwaffe base. On February 7, more than fifty B-17s and B-26s flew north to Sardinia to bomb Elmas Airfield and the seaplane base at Cagliari. Flying north again on February 15, B-17s attacked the harbor and shipping at Palermo, Sicily. Two days later, B-17s returned to Elmas.

On the ground in Tunisia, the U.S. Army had lost its first major engagement with the Afrika Korps on February 19 and 20 at Kasserine Pass. B-17s and other American bombers intervened between February 22 and 24, attacking the German ground troops and Luftwaffe fields, and forcing a German withdrawal that permitted the army to recapture the pass by February 25.

During March, B-17s were tasked with attacking German and Italian shipping in the sea lanes between Sicily and Tunisia, and eight such raids occurred between March 4 and 24. In addition, B-17s struck Tunis on March 3, the marshaling yard at Sousse on March 7 and 12, El Aouina and La Marsa on March 10, and Djebel, Tebaga, and Mezzouna on March 21. On March 31, B-17s targeted Cagliari, Decimomannu, Monserrato, and Villacidro.

April saw the Allies undertake preparations for Operation Husky, the July 1943 invasion of Sicily, as the first step toward taking the war into Italy proper. Accordingly, Allied bombers began targeting ports and railyards in both Sicily and Italy. B-17s attacked both in

A group of Twelfth Air Force airmen out for a camel ride near their base in Tunisia on March 30, 1943, pause to wave to a returning B-17 Flying Fortress. The riders probably staged the scene for the photographer. During World War II, newspapers loved pictures of regular American GIs in exotic locations around the globe.
USAAF via National Archives

the Naples area on April 4, and in Sicily eight times between April 5 and 18. Other B-17 operations during April included a continuation of the campaign against enemy shipping between Italy and North Africa, and strikes against the ports of Tunis and Bizerte.

After a major Allied offensive that got under way at the end of April, the last Axis forces in North Africa finally surrendered on May 13. B-17s made their last raids on the ports of Bizerte and Tunis during the first week of May and then turned their attention to Sicily and beyond. A half dozen attacks in Sicily were conducted between May 6 and May 21. Flying Fortresses struck Naples on the night of May 12 and participated in raids against targets

You should have seen what happened to the other plane! On February 1, 1943, Flying Fortresses of the 414th Bombardment Squadron, 97th Bombardment Group, attacked the German facilities at the port of Tunis, which was then an anchor in the vital supply lifeline for the Afrika Korps. During that operation, experienced Luftwaffe fighter ace Erich Paczia of Jagdgeschwader 53 attacked this B-17F piloted by Kenneth Bragg. Paczia's Messerschmitt Bf.109 struck the Flying Fortress at high speed, nearly slicing off the tail. Paczia's aircraft disintegrated and he was killed, probably by American gunfire before he hit the B-17. Bragg and his crew survived the day. The United States insignia encircled in yellow was used unofficially by many USAAF aircraft in the Mediterranean and European Theaters in late 1942 and early 1943. *USAAF via National Archives*

After being hit by Erich Paczia's Bf.109 over Tunis on February 1, 1943, Kenneth Bragg managed to coax *All American*, his stricken B-17F, back to the Allied air base at Biskra in southern Algeria. Shortly after this picture was taken, the tail collapsed and fell off the airplane. This is one of many testaments to the legendary durability of the Boeing B-17. *USAAF via National Archives*

in Sardinia the same night and again on May 24. B-17s bombed Civitavecchia, north of Rome, on May 14, and the Italian western port city of Livorno on May 28. These were the northernmost attacks on the Italian mainland at that time by B-17s.

The Flying Fortress force in the Mediterranean opened June with raids against Pantelleria Island near Sicily on the first and fourth. Also on the fourth, B-17s headed into northern Italy with an attack on the western port of La Spezia. The railyards at Naples and targets on Sardinia were attacked on June 21. On June 18 and 25, the target was the dock area and railyards at Messina, the Sicilian port nearest to mainland Italy, which was important for bringing supplies and troops into Sicily.

In coordination with the July 10 Operation Husky Allied invasion of Sicily, B-17s were part of an air armada that attacked enemy airfields on the island on June 12 and each day between July 6 and 10. Flying Fortresses continued to work targets on the island through July, including a July 12 attack on the Messina railroad bridges. Later in the month, B-17s also ranged north into mainland Italy, bombing transportation facilities at Naples on July 14 and 17, Bologna on July 24, and Viterbo on July 29. In the meantime, Fascist Italy was imploding. Italian King Vittorio Emanuele III stripped dictator Benito Mussolini of his power on July 25, but continued—albeit temporarily—to wage war against the Allies.

During August, B-17s joined tactical bombers in a continuation against Axis targets on Sicily, especially Messina, through which enemy troops were being evacuated to the mainland. Other Flying Fortress targets for the month included the Capodichino Airfield at Naples on August 3, the submarine base at Naples on August 4, the marshaling yard at Terni in Umbria on August 11, and the marshaling yard at Lorenzi on August 13. On August 25, 135 B-17s and 140 P-38s struck airfields near Foggia, which would later be used by the USAAF to base

This wire photo dated May 21, 1943, shows a B-17 that apparently landed successfully with even more severe tail damage than Kenneth Bragg's *All American*. The similar tail numbers identify both aircraft as Block 5 B-17Fs built in Seattle. *USAAF via National Archives*

B-17s. On August 17, NASAF began attacks on Luftwaffe facilities in southern France when about 180 B-17s struck Salon-de-Provence and Istres, near Marseilles.

On September 3, the Allies began landing troops on mainland Italy, as British forces landed in the toe of the Italian peninsula opposite Messina. Six days later, American forces landed at Salerno, south of Naples, in Operation Avalanche, and additional British forces came ashore at Taranto. On September 8, the Italian government surrendered to the Allies, but that meant only that the Italian army was no longer in play. Most of the resistance faced by the Allies was from German forces, and the Germans seized Italy under a military occupation and continued to fight as before.

The Twelfth Air Force's XII Bomber Command B-17s went into high gear during September, striking communications targets within Italy. On the second, almost 200 Twelfth Air Force B-17s and B-25s struck the marshaling yards at Bologna, Trento, Bolzano, and Cancello Arnone. Three days later, 130 or more B-17s struck the airfield at Viterbo and the town of Civitavecchia. On September 6, the targets were Capodichino Airfield, Villa Literno marshaling yard, Gaeta harbor, and the Minturno railroad facilities, and during the next two days, B-17s hit Foggia and Frascati. On September 9, more than 100 Flying Fortresses struck bridges at Capua and Cancello Arnone,

and on September 11 and 12, the targets were highways and railyards in the Benevento area. B-17s continued to target highway and rail targets nearly every day through September 21, as German troops poured south to wage a counterattack against the Salerno beachhead.

On September 28, B-17s again ranged into northern Italy, with a few bombers striking the Bologna marshaling yard and one hitting Bolzano near the Austrian border. Large forces of B-17s attacked other road and railway targets about twice a week between October 6 and 30.

October also marked the beginning of a B-17 bombing campaign against targets within Germany and Austria from bases in the Mediterranean Theater. On October 1, B-17s attempted a run against Augsburg, but the target was obscured, so they struck alternate targets in Austria, Italy, and off Corsica. On October 27, 150 Twelfth Air Force B-17s and B-24s struck Wiener-Neustadt, near Vienna, and other targets in Austria, including Ebenfurth. Meanwhile, the XII Bomber Command added targets across the Adriatic to the target list during the month. On October 9 and 10, B-17s struck airfields at Larissa, Athens, and Salonika in Greece, and on October 21, rail and road bridges in Albania were hit.

On the first of November, the USAAF activated the Fifteenth Air Force, with the headquarters at Tunis, Tunisia, and Lieutenant General James Doolittle as commanding general. The idea was to transfer all of the heavy bombers from the Twelfth Air Force to the new command. The Fifteenth would then conduct strategic bombing operations as part of the Allied Combined Bomber Offensive. The Fifteenth would be the Mediterranean Theater equivalent of the Britain-based USAAF Eighth Air Force. The Fifteenth was in a better position to hit strategic targets in Austria and southern Germany than was the Eighth. By December 1943, the Fifteenth Air Force began relocating its B-17s and B-24s to bases in Allied-occupied Italy, much closer to the Reich than the bases in North Africa.

On November 1, the Fifteenth Air Force's first day, B-17s struck the town and harbor of La Spezia and a railroad bridge at Vezzano. The following day, it was back to Austria for strategic missions to the Messerschmitt aircraft factory and surrounding industrial complex at Wiener-Neustadt. On November 8, eighty-one Fifteenth Air Force B-17s struck the Villarperosa ball bearing works at Turin and nearby motor and aircraft engine factories

A group of B-17Gs attack an inland target somewhere in German-occupied Europe. *USAAF via National Archives*

in the first of four such missions to be flown through December 1. Other strategic industrial targets included the Genoa-Ansaldo steel works on November 9.

While most tactical missions would be assigned to Twelfth Air Force medium bombers, the Fifteenth's B-17s continued to strike road and rail targets, such as the Fiora River bridge on November 6, the Rimini marshaling yard and bridge on November 26, and the bridges and marshaling yard at Grizzana the next day.

The B-17s ranged far and wide, bombing Istres in France on November 16 and the Luftwaffe base at Eleusis, Greece, twice over the following two days. On November 24, Fifteenth Air Force B-17s attacked both the U-boat base at Toulon, France, and the marshaling yard at Sofia, Bulgaria. The U-boat pens at Marseilles would be a target on December 2.

Also in October and November 1943, Fortress Mk II aircraft serving with the RAF Coastal Command succeeded in sinking German U-boats in the Atlantic.

Fifteenth Air Force B-17s bombed Luftwaffe bases in Greece three times between December 6 and 20, as well as docks and shipping at Piraeus. Two missions were flown against the railyards at Innsbruck, Austria, on December 15 and 19. Meanwhile, targets on the Italian rail network were hit by B-17s on December 15, 16, 25, and 27. The Fifteenth's Flying Fortress force wrapped up the year in the Mediterranean Theater with a December 29 mission against the rail targets at Ferrara and Rimini, and December 30 attacks on marshaling yards at Rimini and Padua.

A split second of a tragedy frozen in time: Probably hit by flak, a B-17G goes down over the target as other Flying Fortresses release their bombs. The fuselage has been consumed by fire, but the wing section is still intact. One of the inboard engines has just fallen off, and its propeller can be seen falling away from the leading edge of the wing. *USAAF via National Archives*

An Eighth Air Force B-17G unloads ordnance on an inland industrial target in German-occupied Europe. *USAAF via National Archives*

B-17F Flying Fortresses of the 390th Bombardment Group head toward the Reich on a cold, but clear, winter's day. The contrails of their escorting fighter aircraft snake dramatically into the skies above. The 390th was based at Framlingham and operational with the Eighth Air Force from July 1943 through the end of the war. *USAAF via National Archives*

CHAPTER FIVE

B-17 OPERATIONS IN 1944

THE EUROPEAN THEATER IN 1944
BEFORE OPERATION OVERLORD

The year 1944 would be the busiest of World War II for the USAAF and the vast B-17 fleet that was concentrated in the air offensive against the Third Reich. The pivotal event of the year in the European Theater would be the Operation Overlord invasion of Normandy on June 6, 1944. During the first half of 1944, all Allied operations were carried out with that invasion in mind. Operation Pointblank—the Combined Bomber Offensive against the Third Reich's infrastructure, industry, and aviation—was executed with an eye toward Overlord.

Despite the heavy losses of late 1943, the USAAF and the RAF remained committed to Pointblank. Plans were also being laid for the biggest air assault to date, an ambitious week-long maximum effort of thousand-plane days that would be called "Big Week."

This was seen as a necessary step in the CBO, because Operation Pointblank was behind schedule. During the latter half of 1943, the monthly average was just seven hundred tons of bombs dropped. The major blow against the German aircraft industry that was the principal goal of

Pointblank required a nearly simultaneous attack on all the major airframe factories. It was hoped that Big Week would come in January, but weather pushed it into February.

Another major management decision made in the first weeks of 1944 was to place the growing fleet of P-51D long-range fighters under the command and control of the Eighth Air Force for escort duty. That meant that heavy bombers flying to targets deep inside the Reich would routinely have the support of a fighter aircraft type that could match the best Luftwaffe interceptors.

The Eighth Air Force began the year with a new commander, as Lieutenant General James Doolittle replaced Lieutenant General Ira Eaker, who was reassigned to Italy as commanding general of the Mediterranean Allied Air Force (MAAF). Meanwhile, the U.S. Strategic Air Forces in Europe (USSAFE, later USSTAF) was created as an umbrella organization to coordinate both the Eighth and Fifteenth Air Forces. In April 1944, the USSTAF, along with all other Allied air, naval, and ground forces in Europe, would be placed under the command of the Supreme Headquarters Allied Expeditionary Force (SHAEF) headed by General Dwight Eisenhower, the supreme allied commander.

The first Eighth Air Force strategic mission of 1944 came on January 4 as 371 B-17s bombed Kiel and 68 hit Munster. The next day, 119 B-17s returned to Kiel as 83 aircraft bombed targets of opportunity and 190 went south to attack Luftwaffe bases in France. On January 7, 351 Flying Fortresses bombed the I.G. Farben factory at Ludwigshafen, and on January 11, 485 B-17s bombed targets within Germany—including Bielefeld, Braunschweig (Brunswick), Halberstadt, Nienburg, Oschersleben, Osnabruck, and Peine—with more than fifty losses.

An indication of the poor weather conditions during the month came on January 24, when 857 B-17s and B-24s launched, and all but 58 were recalled. They bombed a power plant near Eschweiler with the loss of just two. Most of the operations during the month were small leaflet-dropping missions over France. But on January 14 and 21, 356 and 302 B-17s, respectively, flew Operation Crossbow attacks on V-1 cruise missile facilities in France. The weather cleared sufficiently on January 29 for another mission into Germany. Frankfurt was hit by 590 B-17s, while 46 struck Ludwigshafen. The next day, 597 B-17s bombed Braunschweig. On February 10, 141 B-17s again hit Braunschweig.

With Big Week penciled in for the third week of February, the month began for the Eighth Air Force B-17 force on February 3 with 553 of them bombing Wilhelmshaven and another 56 attacking Emden. The next day, 346 B-17s struck Frankfurt, 122 B-17s bombed Giessen, and 51 hit Wiesbaden. On February 5 and 6, seven Luftwaffe facilities in France were targeted in more than 380 B-17 sorties. On February 13, 266 Flying Fortresses attacked V-1 cruise missile sites, joining the B-24s that had been on those targets for much of the month.

B-17s of the 91st Bombardment Group head toward the German port city of Kiel on January 4, 1944. This was the first Eighth Air Force attack of the year against the Third Reich and part of a two-day effort that would see nearly five hundred Flying Fortresses hit Kiel.
USAAF via National Archives

Captain Charles Hudson, a bombardier in an Eighth Air Force B-17G, poses in his plexiglass perch. The shrouded object in front of him is his Norden bombsight. Photographing the Norden was strictly forbidden during World War II. *USAAF via National Archives*

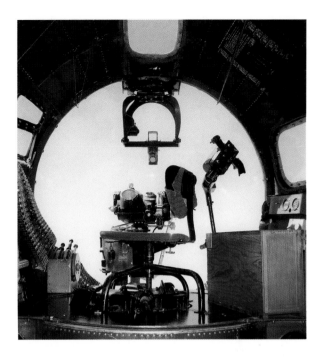

This is the view looking toward the bombardier's station of a B-17G from behind. Taken in the Collings Foundation B-17G after the war, the prohibition against photographing the bombsight was no longer in force. The view from the plexiglass nose of a Flying Fortress was nothing short of spectacular—until the flak started. *Bill Yenne*

Big Week began on Sunday, February 20, 1944, initiating the largest air campaign to date launched against the heart of the Third Reich. The targets on Sunday were German aircraft plants and airfields. One Eighth Air Force wave struck Rostok, while another feinted toward Berlin and then split into two parts. Of them, 417 B-17 Flying Fortresses went after targets in and around Leipzig. Another 239 bombers hit the primary targets at Bernburg and Oschersleben. Meanwhile, 272 B-24 Liberators attacked aviation industry targets at Braunschweig and Neupetritor, while 87 hit Gotha. They were escorted by ninety-four P-38s, 668 Eighth and Ninth Air Force P-47s, and seventy-three Eighth and Ninth Air Force P-51s. The fighter escorts claimed sixty-one Luftwaffe interceptors, but 21 American bombers were lost that day.

On Monday, Big Week continued with 336 Eighth Air Force B-17s attacking the Gutersloh, Lippstadt, and Werl Luftwaffe bases, while 285 bombed Achmer, Bramsche, Diepholz, Hopsten, Lingen, Quakenbruck, and Rheine, as well as the Luftwaffe base at Coevorden in the Netherlands. Another wave included 175 Flying Fortresses

attacking the Diepholz Luftwaffe base and Braunschweig, and 88 bombing Alhorn and Hannover. An additional 244 B-24s attacked the Achmer and Handorf airfields, bringing the total number of heavy bombers to more than eleven hundred.

February 22 found 799 bombers launched against German aviation factories and Luftwaffe airfields. Among these, 181 Eighth Air Force B-17s hit Aschersleben, Bernburg, Bunde, Halberstadt, Magdeburg, Marburg, Wernegerode, and other targets. From that attack, the Luftwaffe claimed 38 B-17s. Another 333 Flying Fortresses set out to attack Schweinfurt, but tempestuous weather forced them to discontinue the mission.

On Wednesday, poor weather conditions created a hiatus in the Big Week attacks on Germany, but on Thursday, 231 Flying Fortresses bombed the ball bearing plants at Schweinfurt, while 238 B-24s hit factories at Gotha and 297 heavy bombers attacked Eisenach and Rostock.

On Friday, February 25, the Eighth Air Force sent 830 bombers and 826 fighters on a three-pronged assault into the Reich. A total of 246 B-17s attacked aviation industry

This B-17 Flying Fortress of the 390th Bombardment Group was part of the strike package that targeted the Messerschmitt Bf.110 assembly plant near Braunschweig (Brunswick) on January 11, 1944. *USAAF via National Archives*

With streaming contrails, a B-17 Flying Fortress of the 91st Bombardment Group heads toward the north German industrial city of Osnabruck on January 18, 1944. *USAAF via National Archives*

targets at Augsburg and the factory area at Stuttgart, while 267 Flying Fortresses hit industry targets at Regensburg. In the third wave, 172 B-24s hit aviation industrial targets at Furth. A total of 31 bombers and three fighter escorts were lost by the Eighth Air Force. Continuing its coordinated attacks with the Eighth Air Force on European targets, the Fifteenth Air Force sent B-17s against Regensburg and against the air depot at Klagenfurt in Austria on Friday.

During Big Week, the USAAF had flown more than thirty-eight hundred daylight fighter and bomber sorties over Germany, while the RAF Bomber Command added an additional twenty-three hundred sorties by night. Almost ten thousand tons of bombs were dropped by the Eighth Air Force in that one week—more than the total that the Eighth had dropped through all of 1943.

Big Week had been an exercise that was carefully planned to use American air power to strike a blow against German air power. Eighth Air Force losses had been severe, but the damage that was done to German industry during Big Week and in succeeding weeks would have a ripple effect that would be felt just over three months later when the Allies came ashore at the beachheads of Normandy.

The Monday morning after Big Week, February 28, 181 Eighth Air Force B-17s bombed Luftwaffe and missile launch facilities in northern France. On the last day of the month, the Eighth returned to the Reich, as 226 B-17s bombed aircraft factories in Braunschweig. On March 2, 204 Flying Fortresses hit the targets around Frankfurt, while 49 bombed Ludwigshafen, 20 bombed Limburg, 12 bombed Fischbach, and 8 hit other targets of opportunity. The same day, 84 B-17s bombed a Luftwaffe base at Chartres in France.

If February was characterized by Big Week, March would see the Eighth Air Force make its first raids on Berlin, and the first raids against the German capital in daylight. An effort launched against Berlin on March 3 was diverted, mainly to Wilhelmshaven, because of weather, but the following day, the Eighth hit Berlin. Weather forced most of the strike package to divert to secondary targets, but 30 Flying Fortresses reached the primary, escorted all the way by P-51D Mustangs. Meanwhile, 100 Flying Fortresses bombed Bonn, 35 bombed Köln, 33 bombed Dusseldorf, 7 bombed Frankfurt, and 33 bombed other targets.

On March 6, the Eighth Air Force launched 504 B-17s and 226 B-24s against Berlin. Of these, 248 B-17s bombed Berlin and 226 hit targets such as Oranienburg, Potsdam, Templin, Verden, and Wittenberg, while 198 B-24s reached Berlin. The Germans did not take the attack on Hitler's capital lightly. The day was characterized by an air-to-air battle of ferocious proportions. The Luftwaffe shot down sixty-nine heavy bombers and eleven fighters—the most that the Eighth Air Force had lost in a single day. Meanwhile, though, the bomber gunners and the Mustang pilots destroyed at least ninety-seven Luftwaffe interceptors.

Two days later, the Eighth Air Force returned to Berlin with 320 B-17s and 150 B-24s hitting their primary targets. That time, the Eighth lost thirty-seven bombers and sixteen fighters while downing sixty-three enemy planes. On March 9, the target again was Berlin, as 339 B-17s hit the capital with only six losses.

On March 11, Munster was the target for 120 Flying Fortresses, and on March 13, 127 B-17s joined B-24s in attacks against fixed missile-launch facilities in France. March 15 and 16 saw an average of 293 B-17s bomb targets in Braunschweig and Augsburg, while 46 struck nearby Gessertshausen and 18 bombed Ulm.

On March 18, Luftwaffe bases and aircraft factories headed the target list, as 480 B-17s bombed Landsberg,

Lechfeld, Memmingen, Munich, and Oberpfaffenhofen. Two days later, weather prevented all but 146 B-17s from getting through to targets such as Frankfurt and Mannheim. On the intervening day of March 19, 173 Flying Fortresses hit V-1 facilities in France.

March 22 saw Flying Fortresses over Berlin for the first time in about two weeks, as 460 B-17s, tasked with hitting factories at Oranienburg and Basdorf, diverted to the capital. The next day, weather again was a factor, as 205 B-17s bombed Braunschweig, while 219 diverted to secondary targets at Ahlen, Hamm, Munster, Neubeckum, and elsewhere. Schweinfurt, and its notorious ball bearing industry, was in the Eighth Air Force crosshairs for March 24, and 60 B-17s reached the primary, while 162 bombed the Frankfurt marshaling yard.

During the three days beginning on March 26, a daily average of 423 Flying Fortresses hit myriad targets, mainly Luftwaffe facilities, across northern France from Calais to Cherbourg, and deep within France as far south as Dijon and Bordeaux. Another such attack on targets across northern France would occur on April 20 and involve 438 B-17s.

On March 29, the Eighth Air Force began nearly a month of focus on Luftwaffe bases and German industrial targets, with 233 B-17s hitting Braunschweig, Unterluss, Stedorf, and other targets. April opened with a week of weather-related delays, but 309 B-17s were active against Luftwaffe bases on April 8, targeting Oldenburg, Achmer, Quakenbruck, Rheine, Enschede, Hesepe, Handorf, and other locations. The next day, 273 B-17s hit aircraft factories and fields in Germany and Poland at Marienberg, Marienehe, Poznan, Rahmel, and Warnemunde. On April 10, the targets were factories and fields in France and the Low Countries at Beaumont sur Oise, Bergen op Zoom, Brussels, Courcelles, Diest, Evere, Florennes, and Maldagem.

On April 11 and 13, the Eighth Air Force flew a maximum effort against industrial targets within Germany, involving a daily average of 483 B-17s along with a sizable number of B-24s. Schweinfurt's ball bearing industry and other targets, mainly aircraft factories, were attacked in Arnimswalde, Augsburg, Cottbus, Politz, Rostock, Stettin, and Trechel. A third mission on April 12 was aborted because of weather. Another two-day campaign against Luftwaffe-related targets with Germany began on April 18 and involved a daily average of nearly 500 B-17s. The target list included Brandenburg, Eschwege, Kassel, Lippstadt, Luneburg, Oranienburg, Perleberg, Rathenow, Werl, and Wittenberg.

Posing jauntily with his silk scarf and bomber jacket, First Lieutenant Willis Kennedy was a Flying Fortress pilot with the 381st Bombardment Group, based at Ridgewell, England, in 1944. *USAAF via National Archives*

Late in April, Eighth Air Force targeting expanded to highlight Germany's petroleum industry. Though aircraft targets would remain high on the list, all damage done to Germany's ability to refine, store, and transport petroleum products would impact its ability to wage war on many levels. The effort began on April 22, with 474 Flying Fortresses hitting Hamm and 39 attacking Bonn and Soest. Two days later, aircraft-related targets in and around Erding, Friedrichshafen,

Flying Fortresses of the 457th Bombardment Group open their bomb bays during their final run over Munster on March 11, 1944. They were among 120 B-17s to strike this Westphalian industrial city on that date. *USAAF via National Archives*

Landsberg, Neckarsulm, and Oberpfaffenhofen were struck by 442 B-17s.

On April 25, 27, 28, and 30, a daily average of 223 B-17s attacked the Luftwaffe bases at Avord, Clermont-Ferrand, Dijon, LeCulot, Lyon, Metz, Nancy, and Toul in France, as well as one near Ostend, Belgium. April 26 saw 339 B-17s back over Germany, hitting targets in and around Braunschweig, Hildesheim, and Hannover.

On April 28, eighteen Flying Fortresses struck a missile facility near Sottevast in France, which, like Watten, was intended for V-2 ballistic missiles rather than V-1 cruise missiles.

Berlin was the target for the first time in more than a month on April 29, as 368 Flying Fortresses hit the German capital and 34 bombed Magdeburg and Brandenburg. The renewed Berlin campaign was to have continued on May 4, but weather caused most of the planes to abort and 40 B-17s to divert to the Bergen Luftwaffe base in the Netherlands. On May 7, the Flying Fortresses got through to the German capital, with 514 striking the primary targets in Berlin and 39 bombing targets of opportunity. The next day, 386 B-17s bombed Berlin and 59 struck Braunschweig. On May 19, 495 B-17s attacked Berlin, as 49 of the same strike package hit Kiel. The next and last B-17 Berlin mission for the month came on May 24, as 464 bombed the primary, 34 struck Nauen, and 13 hit Rechlin.

On May 12, the strategic mission against petroleum facilities was addressed against targets in Germany and Czechoslovakia. Mersenburg was bombed by 224 B-17s, while 140 hit Brux. Another 207 hit other targets, including Chemnitz, Gera, Hof, Lutzkendorf, and Zwickau. The next day, 451 Flying Fortresses bombed Osnabruck, Stettin, and Stralsund. On May 22, 289 B-17s bombed Kiel.

In addition to the Berlin missions and the other large raids inside Germany, May saw many of Eighth Air Force operations going into softening up northern France for the invasion, and the continuing Operation Crossbow missions against the missile sites. On May 1, 268 B-17s operating in groups of about 40 hit targets that included Metz, Montdidier, Poix, Reims, Roye, Saarguemines, and Troyes in France, as well as Brussels in Belgium. On May 8, ninety-two Flying Fortresses hit Crossbow targets at Sottevast and elsewhere. The next day, 456 B-17s struck targets at Chievres, Juvincourt, Laon, Lille, Luxembourg, Saint-Dizier, and Thionville. On May 11, 609 B-17s escorted by 471 fighters were sent to bomb marshaling yards across Belgium, France, Germany, and Luxembourg

The crew of the Eighth Air Force B-17G *Button Nose* is seen here with the bomber at USAAF Station 167 near Ridgewell, England. This Flying Fort was assigned to the 535th Bombardment Squadron of the 381st Bombardment Group in 1944. From left to right, those in the foreground are Technical Sergeant Alfred Haugen (top gunner), First Lieutenant C. J. Robertson (navigator), T. G. "Tail-End Charlie" Bowmer (tail gunner), Lieutenant Charles W. Nevins (bombardier), Technical Sergeant Melvin Samuels (radio operator), and Staff Sergeant William A. Karcher (ball turret gunner). Standing, from left to right, are Staff Sergeant Emory Harris (left waist gunner), Lieutenant W. A. Schubert (co-pilot), Lieutenant T. E. Barnicle (command pilot), and Staff Sergeant E. G. Graybill. *USAAF, author collection*

in anticipation of Operation Overlord, which was less than a month away.

May 15 and 21 saw sixty-three B-17 missions against missile sites in France, and on May 20, 288 B-17s renewed the campaign against Luftwaffe facilities in France. Between May 23 and 25, more than seven hundred Flying Fortress missions were flown against Luftwaffe bases, marshaling yards, and other targets across northern France and Belgium, as well as in Saarbrucken and Neunkirchen in Germany.

On May 27, marshaling yards in Germany were targeted, with Ludwigshafen hit by 150 bombers, Mannheim by 125, and Karlsruhe by 98. Other targets in Germany were hit by 43 Flying Fortresses, and 138 Flying Fortresses bombed targets in France, especially Strasbourg.

Petroleum, factory, and rail targets were on the list May 28 as 477 B-17s bombed Bohlen, Brandis, Camburg, Dessau, Frankfurt, Gera, Köln, Konigsburg, Leipzig, Magdeburg, Meissen, Ruhland, Ubigau, and Zwickau. Over the next two days, Flying Fortress missions were flown against aircraft industry targets at Cottbus, Dessau, Halberstadt, Krzesinki, Leipzig, Oschersleben, Posen, and Sorau.

The last two days of the month saw seventy-six B-17s completing an Operation Crossbow mission, and a total of 513 Flying Fortress sorties flown against Luftwaffe bases and marshaling yards, from Reims and Troyes in France to Osnabruck in Germany. The pace of such missions was building toward a crescendo as D-day approached.

THE MEDITERRANEAN THEATER OF OPERATIONS BEFORE OVERLORD

As noted earlier, 1944 would be the busiest year of World War II for the USAAF B-17 fleet. The central milestone of the year in the European Theater would be Operation Overlord, and the Mediterranean Theater would be peripherally involved with Overlord preparations because of its proximity to France. Coincidentally, one of the biggest events in the Mediterranean Theater would be the fall of Rome to the Allies on June 5, 1944, just one day before Overlord.

Of course, there would be a blurring of theater boundaries for USAAF bomber operations because 1944 would also see routine missions flown from the Mediterranean Theater against many of the same targets within Germany that were being attacked by bombers flying from Britain in the European Theater.

Effective on the first day of 1944, the U.S. Strategic Air Forces in Europe (USSAFE) was created as the umbrella organization to coordinate the operations of the Britain-based Eighth Air Force and the Mediterranean-based Fifteenth Air Force as the USAAF contribution to the Combined Bomber Offensive (CBO). General Carl Spaatz served as USSAFE commander. Two days after the creation of USSAFE, General Nathan Twining took over as commander of the Fifteenth Air Force. Within a week, the Fifteenth would consist of eight heavy bomber groups, all of which were based within Italy soon thereafter. Within the next ninety days, the number of groups had doubled to sixteen. The planned operational strength of twenty-one groups would be reached on May 10.

This excellent underside view of a 452nd Bombardment Group B-17G shows the aircraft with its bomb bay open as it prepares to unload its ordnance over Berlin early in 1944. *USAAF via National Archives*

The CBO target list was headed by vital industrial plants, lines of communication, and the Luftwaffe. The list focused on targets that could be struck decisively.

During January, Fifteenth Air Force B-17s would average one raid every second day against road, rail, and airfield targets within Italy at locations ranging from Perugia to Florence. On January 3, the Fifteenth began the year with a raid on Turin-area industrial targets such as the Villarperosa ball bearing works, the Lingotto marshaling yard, and the Fiat motor vehicle factory. The next day, more than 100 B-17s were sent to strike the Dupnica area of Bulgaria. Of those, 29 struck the target area, but heavy cloud cover caused 77 B-17s to return with their bombs undropped.

The Fifteenth was also active against German forces and infrastructure outside Italy and the Reich. Flying Fortresses ranged throughout southern Europe. On January 9, B-17s bombed the docks and shipping at Pula, Yugoslavia (now Pula, Croatia), and the following day B-17s struck the marshaling yards at Sofia, Bulgaria,

This B-17G of the 486th Bombardment Group was one of 486 Flying Fortresses dispatched by the Eighth Air Force on April 10, 1944, against aircraft factories and Luftwaffe fields across France and the low countries. The largest number attacked various targets in the Brussels vicinity. Only two B-17s were lost that day. *USAAF via National Archives*

causing considerable damage. Approximately sixty Luftwaffe fighters intercepted them, and 2 B-17s were lost. The bomber force reported twenty-eight enemy aircraft shot down. On January 11, Flying Fortresses, with P-38 escorts, struck the harbor at Piraeus, Greece, but 6 B-17s were lost in midair collisions in the heavy overcast conditions. Three days later, approximately 200 B-24s and B-17s struck the town area and airfield at Mostar, Yugoslavia.

On January 16, and again on January 31, B-17s crossed the Alps to bomb the Messerschmitt factory at Klagenfurt, Austria. On January 21, Fifteenth Air Force B-17s struck airfields at Istres and Salon-de-Provence in France, and three days later, B-17s bombed the marshaling yard at Vrattsa and the Dolno Tserovene area in Bulgaria.

During the first half of February, bad weather hampered operations, including a February 4 attack on the Toulon harbor in France and various missions within Italy. February 14 was a big day, as B-17s struck the marshaling yards at Modena, Brescia, and Verona and several targets of opportunity, including the airfield and Piaggio aircraft factory at Pontedera, and railroad bridges and lines south of Vicenza and at Parma, Sassuolo, and Rubiera.

The following day, B-17s turned to tactical targets, specifically German positions at the Monte Cassino Benedictine Abbey—then the scene of a vicious ground battle. On March 15, B-17s would return to Cassino, which the Germans had turned into the major fortress anchoring their Gustav Line.

On February 17, B-17s and B-24s struck Campoleone and Grottaferrata, as well as targets in advance of the U.S. Fifth Army's Anzio battle line, which was under heavy counterattack by German forces. On February 22, the B-17s targeted strategic areas related to aircraft production, including the factories within Germany at Regensburg and the Luftwaffe depot at Zagreb in Yugoslavia. Three days later, Flying Fortresses returned to Regensburg, while other B-17s bombed the air depot at Klagenfurt and the dock area at Pola.

On March 2, nearly 300 B-17s and B-24s again flew in support of the Anzio beachhead, bombing troop concentrations, guns, and other military targets at several points in the area south of Rome. The next day, it was back to the strategic mission with B-17s bombing marshaling yards at Rome, Littorio, and Tiburtina. On March 7, the B-17s targeted the U-boat base at Toulon, and on March 11, more than 100 B-17s bombed the marshaling yard at Padua. March 19 saw 234 B-17s and B-24s strike Klagenfurt, and around 100 B-17s struck the marshaling

Posing like a Hollywood leading man, Technical Sergeant Vernon Lindemeyer was a gunner aboard a B-17 assigned to the 381st Bombardment Group. *USAAF via National Archives*

yards at Verona three days later. On March 26, B-17s struck the Fiume docks.

The three days between March 28 and 30 saw the largest Fifteenth Air Force strikes to date. On the first day, more than 400 B-17s bombed targets in Mestre, Verona, and elsewhere in northern Italy. On the second day, a like number of bombers were launched, with the B-17s striking factories and railyards at Turin. On March 30, nearly 350 B-17s and B-24s struck marshaling yards at Sofia and an industrial complex and airfield at Imotski, Yugoslavia.

On April 2, with sixteen heavy bomber groups operational, the Fifteenth Air Force launched 530 B-24s and B-17s against targets in Austria and Yugoslavia, with the B-17s bombing a ball bearing plant at Steyr, Austria, and the marshaling yard at Brod, Yugoslavia. The next day, 450 or more B-17s and B-24s struck targets in Hungary and Yugoslavia, with the B-17s targeting an aircraft factory in Budapest and the marshaling yard at Brod.

Three of the next four days also saw maximum-effort missions, each averaging between 300 and 400 B-17s and

This B-17F, tail number 41-24577, was named *Hell's Angels* after the 1930 Howard Hughes movie about World War I fighter pilots. Assigned to the 358th Bombardment Squadron of the 303rd Bombardment Group, this Flying Fortress was originally commanded by Captain Irl E. Baldwin. He piloted her overseas from Kellogg Field near Battle Creek, Michigan, to Molesworth, England, in 1942. The bomber would fly with several commanders and numerous crewmen during her fifteen months with the Eighth Air Force in the European Theater. She is seen here having completed her thirty-first mission. *USAAF via National Archives*

B-24s. The B-17s attacked Bucharest, Romania, on April 4, Ploesti on April 5, and Treviso on April 7. After several days of bad weather, a 450-plane mission went out on April 12, with the B-17s hitting aircraft factories at Fischamend in Austria and Split in Yugoslavia. The next day marked another record day, with 535 heavy bombers sent against targets in Hungary.

On April 15, 448 B-17s and B-24s went out, with the former striking marshaling yards at Ploesti and Nis, Yugoslavia. The next two days saw 432 and 470 heavy bombers launched, with the B-17s striking Belgrade, Yugoslavia, and an aircraft plant at Brasov, Romania. On April 20, more than 300 B-17s and B-24s attacked targets in Italy, with the B-17s targeting marshaling yards at Ancona, Castelfranco, Padua, Vicenza, and the Venice harbor. On April 23, the targets for 500 or more B-17s and B-24s were aircraft facilities in Austria, with the B-17s bombing the Wiener Neustadt industrial area. The next day, 520 or more bombers were launched, with the B-17s

attacking a marshaling yard at Ploesti, an aircraft factory in Belgrade, and the Ancona-Rimini railroad line.

On April 28, 188 B-17s struck the steel mill and port at Piombino, Italy, and the next day 573 B-17s were sent against the naval base at Toulon. A similar number went out on the last day of the month, bombing industrial areas at Milan and Varese, as well as the Reggio Emilia air depot.

The first day of May found B-17s hitting the marshaling yard at Bolzano as part of a 250-bomber package. May 5 saw another record-size mission, with 640 bombers going out. The B-17 contingent bombed marshaling yards at Ploesti and Brasov. The next day, a force half that size was launched, and the B-17s returned to Brasov.

On May 10, as the Fifteenth Air Force reached its planned operational strength of twenty-one bomber groups, approximately four hundred bombers crossed the Alps to target Wiener Neustadt, but weather forced three hundred of the bombers to abort, and twenty-one were lost. Two days later, there was a switch to a tactical rather

The Flying Fortress *Hell's Angels* in January 1944, having completed forty-eight total bombing missions. Tasked with returning to the United States for a war bond tour, the B-17F was autographed by hundreds of 303rd Bombardment Group ground and flight crew personnel at Molesworth. On January 20, with Captain John M. Johnson at the controls, she headed west. Nine days later, Captain Irl Baldwin, her original commander, took the controls for the war bond tour to eighteen American cities. The tour culminated at March Field near Riverside, California, in May, and *Hell's Angels* became a crew training aircraft. She was scrapped before the war ended. Oft-repeated speculation that the motorcycle club of the same name was founded by former crewmen of *Hell's Angels* is erroneous. *USAAF via National Archives*

Some of the most challenging flying faced by B-17 crews over Europe during World War II were the missions flown across the Alps by crews of the Fifteenth Air Force—especially during the winter. *USAAF via National Archives*

The B-17G *2nd Patches* flew with the 346th Bombardment Squadron of the 99th Bombardment Group, based at Tortorella, Italy, from August 1943 though the end of the war. She reportedly crashed on takeoff in August 1944 and was salvaged. *USAAF via National Archives*

Clad in fleece-lined leather high-altitude gear, waist gunners in a B-17E aim their weapons and scan the sky for enemy interceptors. This is probably a staged demonstration photo, not one taken in combat. Nevertheless, the two gunners are playing their roles well.
Boeing

than strategic mission. On that day, a record force of around 730 B-17s and B-24s went out to hit targets throughout Italy. Among the targets were the German headquarters at Massa d'Albe and Monte Soratte, the town of Civitavecchia, Orbetello Island, Piombino harbor, Chiavari, La Spezia, and San Stefano al Mare. Also on the long target list that day were Luftwaffe bases at Tarquinia and the marshaling yards at Chivasso, Piombino, Marina di Carrara, Viareggio, and Ferrara.

On May 13, the Fifteenth Air Force continued the tactical mission against the Italian rail network, with about 670 B-17s and B-24s going after widely dispersed targets at Avisio, Bologna, Bolzano, Borgo San Lorenzo, Bronzola, Castel Maggiore, Cesena, Faenza, Fidenza, Imola, Modena, Parma, Piacenza, San Rufillo, and Trento. The next day, more than 700 heavy bombers attacked similar targets, with the B-17s bombing marshaling yards at Ferrara and Mantua and a Luftwaffe depot at Piacenza. A 450-plane raid on May 17 saw B-17s strike the marshaling yard at Ancona and troop concentrations at Bihac, Yugoslavia. The day after, nearly 450

heavy bombers went east, with the B-17s hitting Ploesti, Belgrade, and the marshaling yard at Nis, Yugoslavia.

On May 19, about 500 bombers hit targets across Italy, with B-17s bombing oil storage facilities at Porto Marghera and railroad bridges at Casarea, Latisana, and Rimini. Three days later, B-17s were part of a 550-plane package that bombed the marshaling yard at Avezzano. On May 23, over 300 B-17s and B-24s attacked troop concentrations and communications targets at Avezzano, Grottaferrata, Marino, Nemi, Subiaco, and Valmontone.

On May 24, the Fifteenth Air Force was back on the strategic mission, and the B-17 contingent of a 620-bomber mission went after targets that included the aircraft components factory in Atzgersdorf, Austria. The next day, the B-17s struck the marshaling yard at Lyon, France, and on May 26, almost 700 bombers were launched with B-17s bombing the marshaling yard at Avignon. Seven hundred bombers again took off on May 27, and the B-17s struck the marshaling yard at Saint-Etienne, France.

A new record number of Fifteenth Air Force bombers—829—were sent out to hit strategic targets on

May 29. Only three more times would the Fifteenth Air Force dispatch more than 800 bombers, and two of those missions would be in the last month of the war. For the B-17s, the target was the aircraft factory at Wollesdorf, Austria. The last two days of the month would see the Fifteenth Air Force launch a daily average of nearly 500 bombers, and the B-17s struck the marshaling yard at Zagreb on May 30. Both the B-17s and B-24s hit oil refineries and communications targets in the Ploesti area on May 31.

During the first five months of 1944, the Fifteenth Air Force came into being and nearly tripled in size. As the year began, getting one hundred planes out on a mission was a big deal. By the eve of Operation Overlord, missions on a scale four or five times that size were routine, and an armada in excess of seven hundred planes in one day was no longer front-page news.

THE EUROPEAN THEATER OF OPERATIONS FROM OVERLORD TO COBRA

The most important moment of 1944 in the European Theater would be the Operation Overlord invasion of northern France. It would be the largest single military operation of the war, and all of the resources under the command of the Supreme Headquarters

Seen over a target in the spring of 1944, *Joker* was a Seattle-built Block 25 B-17G assigned to the 774th Bombardment Squadron of the 463rd Bombardment Group and based at Celone, Italy. The six Fifteenth Air Force Flying Fortress Bombardment Groups all carried a "Y" tail code, but each group was distinguished by the shape of the shield that carried the tail code. The 463rd's was shaped like a pie slice. *Joker* was reported lost over Blechhammer in the summer of 1944. *USAAF via National Archives*

Allied Expeditionary Force (SHAEF), including the heavy bomber force of the U.S. Strategic Air Forces in Europe, would be focused on ensuring the success of the mission.

For the Eighth Air Force, it would mean a continued attack against rail and road transportation to—in the words of contemporary tasking orders—"isolate the battlefield." Attacks also proceeded against Luftwaffe facilities and coastal defenses. The missions would continue to occupy about half of the resources of the Eighth through July 25—the date of Operation Cobra, the American breakout from the Normandy beachhead area.

Prior to Operation Overlord, Eighth Air Force isolate-the-battlefield targets were located in the Pas de Calais area of northeastern France. It was not the actual landing zone, but, being closest to England, it was the most logical landing zone. The Allies had been trying hard to convince German planners that they intended to land there, not farther west in Normandy. They were successful: When the invading troops landed in Normandy, the Germans continued to believe that the landing was a diversion and that the real invasion would come at Calais. The diversionary attacks flown by Allied bombers were known as Operation Cover.

D-day for Overlord was June 5, although bad weather on that date would postpone it for a day. General Eisenhower was sure that June 6 would work after he had weather reports brought to him by B-17s flying weather reconnaissance missions over the Atlantic for several days before D-day.

D-day coincided with the 493rd Bombardment Group (Heavy) becoming operational, which brought the Eighth to its peak strength of forty heavy bomber groups.

On June 2, the Flying Fortresses of the Eighth began their Overlord support mission by flying 163 sorties against rail targets near Paris, while 62 other B-17s bombed Luftwaffe bases. They flew 521 Operation Crossbow missions that morning against missile facilities in the Pas de Calais area. On June 3 and 4, 316 and 405 B-17s, respectively, struck coastal defenses in the Pas de Calais. Also on June 4, 630 B-17s reached deeper into France to hit crucial targets, such as railway junctions, bridges, and Luftwaffe bases at or near Avord, Bretigny, Bourges, Massey, Melun, Romorantin, Versailles, and Villeneuve. On June 5, with Overlord postponed until the next day, 423 B-17s and 203 B-24s bombed coastal defenses in the major French ports of Boulogne, Caen, Cherbourg, and Le Havre.

A Fifteenth Air Force B-17G releases a string of five-hundred-pound high-explosive bombs against a target in northern Italy. *USAAF via National Archives*

Just before dawn on D-day, 659 B-17s and 418 B-24s bombed coastal targets throughout the Overlord landing zone from Le Havre to Cherbourg. As the troops began to come ashore, the heavy bombers went deep, and 325 B-17s hit communications targets at Argentan, Conde-sur-Noireau,

A pair of Flying Fortresses over the English countryside of Essex in early 1944. Both were assigned to the 533rd Bombardment Squadron of the 381st Bombardment Group. The one in the foreground is *Princess Pat*, a Block 15 Lockheed-Vega-built B-17G in factory-applied camouflage paint. The bomber in the background is a Block 10 Douglas-built B-17G in natural metal finish. *USAAF via National Archives*

Coutances, Falaise, Lisieux, Pont-l'Eveque, Saint-Lôô, Thury-Harcourt, and Vire. On the morning of June 7, despite poor weather, 172 B-17s continued to isolate the battlefields with runs against additional targets in the same vicinity. In the afternoon, 230 B-17s hit Nantes, while another 231 attacked other targets that included Luftwaffe bases. The next day, nearly 400 B-17s reached farther inland, striking La Frilliere, Orleans, Rennes, and Tours.

On June 9, bad weather precluded air operations over France. But on the next day, 298 B-17s attacked Berck, Equihen-Plage, Gael, Hardelot, Merlimont-Plage, Nantes, Saint-Gabriel, Vannes, and other targets.

Operations against Germany were to resume on June 11, but for four days, beginning on that date, weather diverted the bombers back to France. In that period, 1,663 B-17 sorties hit Luftwaffe facilities at places such as Beaumont-sur-Oise, Beaumont-le-Roger, Beauvais, Berck, Bernay, Bretigny, Conches, Coulommiers, Creil, Dinard, Dreux, Etampes, Evreux, Le Bourget, Melun, Merlimont, Pontaubault, Saint-Andre de L'Eure, Toucquet-Paris-Plage, as well as bridges around Rennes and Saint-Nazaire. On June 14, 243 B-17s also hit Luftwaffe targets in Belgium at Brussels, Florennes, Le Culot, and the famous night fighter (*nachtjaeger*) base at Saint-Trond (Sint Truiden).

On June 15, the B-17s finally returned to strategic targets in Germany, as 172 Flying Fortresses bombed the Hannover/Misburg oil refinery, 16 bombed Wilster, 16 bombed Wesermunde, 2 bombed the Hannover area, and one attacked Helgoland Island. Meanwhile, France continued to figure on the target list as 144 B-17s bombed the Bordeaux/Merignac Luftwaffe base, 127 bombed Nantes railroad bridges, 71 bombed the La Poissonniere rail viaduct, 70 bombed the Angouleme marshaling yard, and 12 bombed the Gael Luftwaffe base.

During June and July, the missile sites in northern France would also be an extremely important target. Their significance was underscored on the night of June 13, when the Germans were finally able to begin V-1 operations against England. With the cruise missiles then impacting London and other British cities, the Operation Crossbow attacks had renewed purpose. Both heavy and medium bombers were involved.

In addition to other missions into France, there were more than 1,500 B-17 Operation Crossbow sorties flown between June 15 and July 17, plus another 334 during August. The highlight came on July 6, when 714 Flying Fortresses attacked the V-1 sites. By mid-September, the

A B-17F unloads its ordnance over an enemy target on D-day, June 6, 1944, the day that the Allies launched their Operation Overlord invasion of continental Europe. Eighth Air Force Flying Fortresses were pressed into service to "isolate the battlefield" by attacking German transportation routes leading to the front. *USAAF via National Archives*

Allies had captured the areas of northern France where the launch sites were located, and the V-1 threat was over.

Germany itself, mainly the petroleum industry, was again targeted on June 18, and 527 Flying Fortresses struck Hamburg, 148 bombed Hannover, and 103 hit Bremen. However, most of the Eighth Air Force's attention between June 16 and 19 was on isolating the battlefield in France, as 491 Flying Fortress sorties struck rail and Luftwaffe facilities in places such as Bordeaux, Cabanac, Cazaux, Chateaudun, Cormes Ecluse, Juvincourt, L'Eveque, Landes-de-Bussac, Laon, Monchy-Breton, Noyen, and Villiers.

On June 20, the Eighth Air Force turned again to strategic targets in northern Germany, with 296 Flying Fortresses bombing Brunsbuttel, Fallersleben, Magdeburg, and Konigsberg, while 403 attacked petroleum facilities around Hamburg. The next day, 559 B-17s attacked Berlin and 85 bombed Basdorf and other targets.

It was also on June 21 that the Eighth Air Force began Operation Frantic, the so-called "shuttle bombing" missions, which involved striking targets deep inside eastern Europe that were beyond the roundtrip range possible from bases in England. After their missions, the bombers would land and refuel inside the Soviet Union. The Fifteenth Air Force had begun shuttle bombing on June 2. Three weeks later, the Eighth's first Frantic mission saw 145 Flying Fortresses bomb the synthetic petroleum factory at Ruhland and other targets. That night, the Luftwaffe attacked the bombers at their Soviet landing field, destroying 47.

On June 26, seventy-two of the B-17s took off from Soviet fields, struck targets at Drohobycz in Poland, and flew south to Fifteenth Air Force bases in Italy. On July 3, fifty-five of the aircraft joined Fifteenth Air Force bombers in a strike against marshaling yards at Arad in Romania. On July 5, seventy Operation Frantic B-17s struck a marshaling yard at Beziers in France with Fifteenth Air Force B-24s. Over the following few days, the Frantic Flying Fortresses gradually returned to England.

Between June 22 and July 17, in the isolating-the-battlefield campaign, more than twenty-eight hundred Eighth Air Force B-17 sorties attacked targets across northern

Journalist Walter Cronkite and B-17 pilot Captain R. W. Sheets prepare for a flight over the Operation Overlord invasion beaches on June 6, 1944. Having joined United Press in 1937, Cronkite became one of the leading American war correspondents in World War II, covering battles in North Africa and Europe. He was also one of the first journalists to fly multiple B-17 missions over Germany. During the war, he was recruited by Edward R. Murrow to join CBS radio news. He transferred to CBS television in 1950 and anchored the CBS Evening News from 1962 to 1981. *USAAF via National Archives*

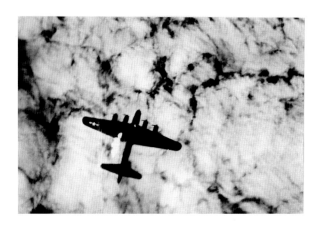

Trailing fire from its number two engine, this B-17 Flying Fortress manages to maintain level flight. With a fire like this, the aircraft is doomed. One hopes there was enough level flight time to permit the crew to get out. *USAAF via National Archives*

France and neighboring Belgium. (This total excludes Operation Crossbow and the nocturnal leaflet-dropping missions that were flown by about 6 B-17s several times each week.) The peak days during those three weeks were July 25 and 26, when 496 and 485 B-17s, respectively, attacked Luftwaffe bases and transportation lines, and July 8, when a total of 568 Flying Fortresses hit their targets. On some days, more than a dozen separate targets were struck. The focus on July 5 was the Netherlands, as 77 B-17s hit Luftwaffe facilities, including Gilze-Rijen, Volkel, and Noll.

The Eighth Air Force celebrated Bastille Day, July 14, by sending 319 B-17s deep into France to drop thirty-seven

A B-17G Flying Fortress of the 492nd Bombardment Group releases its ordnance over the target. *USAAF via National Archives*

hundred containers of supplies to the Françaises de l'Intérior (French Forces of the Interior), the underground resistance within France.

Meanwhile, the strategic campaign against the Reich itself continued. On June 24, 253 Flying Fortresses bombed targets in Bremen, while 53 bombed an aircraft plant at Westermunde. Five days later, 89 B-17s hit Leipzig, 81 struck the synthetic petroleum factory at Bohlen, 79 attacked Wittenberg, 15 bombed Limbach, and 16 bombed Quackenbruck and targets of opportunity.

On July 7, another big raid into Germany put 308 B-17s over the Leipzig area, while 64 bombed Bohlen, 51

Staff Sergeant G. S. McCall explains the nuances of his B-17G's Wright R1820-97 Cyclone radial engine to a pair of jolly young Soviet soldiers and their political commissar. The commissars distrusted the Yanks, but they distrusted their own troops more. Though the big news during June 1944 was Operation Overlord, the month also marked the beginning of Operation Frantic. The operation involved USAAF heavy bombers from both the Eighth Air Force and the Fifteenth Air Force attacking targets in the far eastern parts of German-occupied Europe and then landing at bases in Soviet Russia. The targets were too far for round-trip missions from Italy or England, and bases in Russia made them possible. During the war, the Soviet Red Army had a much higher percentage of women in combat roles than any other nation. *USAAF via National Archives*

bombed Merseburg petroleum factories, 102 bombed Kolleda, 32 bombed Lutzkendorf Luftwaffe bases, 16 bombed Gottingen marshaling yard, and 29 bombed other targets.

July 11 began a three-day maximum effort against Munich, which had received relatively little attention to that point from the Eighth Air Force because it was deep in southern Germany and a long flight from England. On that day, 660 Flying Fortresses bombed the targets in and around the Bavarian capital. On July 12, the Eighth Air Force launched 1,271 heavy bombers, of which 1,124 succeeded in attacking Munich. On July 13, 495 Flying Fortresses hit Munich in two waves. By that time, it was possible for the Eighth Air Force to send a mixed force of more than a thousand B-17s and B-24s over Germany on a single day.

On July 16, Munich was revisited by 213 B-17s, while 258 bombed Stuttgart, 54 bombed Augsburg, and 52 bombed other targets. Two days later, the focus shifted to northern Germany as twenty-six Flying Fortresses bombed Kiel, Cuxhaven, and other targets. Also on July 16, 377 B-17s attacked the German experimental station at Peenemunde on the Baltic coast, home of the V-2 ballistic missile test program. The following day, 1,082 B-17s and B-24s, operating in five detachments, hit targets across southern Germany, again including Munich. The raids against the latter city were timed so that the bombers would be followed in ninety minutes by a wave of Fifteenth Air Force heavy bombers coming up from the south.

On July 20—the same day that members of Hitler's own officer corps attempted unsuccessfully to assassinate him—

Chief Master Sergeant Roberts directs a 381st Bombardment Group B-17G to hold for takeoff at the USAAF base near Ridgewell, England. *USAAF via National Archives*

the Eighth Air Force added insult to injury by sending 417 B-17s against targets in Germany at Bitterfeld, Dessau, Giessen, Kolleda, Kothen, Leipzig, Lutzkendorf, Merseburg, Nordhuasen, Rudolstadt, and Wetzlar. The next day, 192 B-17s bombed targets in and around Regensburg and Stuttgart, while a separate wave put 99 Flying Fortresses over Schweinfurt and another 168 over Bad Kreuznach, Ebelsbach, Ludwigshafen, and other targets.

With those missions, the Eighth Air Force paused in its attacks on Germany to prepare for what would be one of its most concentrated tactical missions ever: ground support in advance of Operation Cobra.

The Allied ground forces that came ashore on D-day had been bogged down for seven weeks, contained by the German armies in a narrow strip of Normandy. Operation Cobra would be the long-awaited breakout. SHAEF planned to launch a massive ground assault in the wake of a massive air assault by an armada of bombers as big as the Eighth could launch. D-day for Cobra was July 24, but like Overlord, it would be delayed 24 hours, although the Eighth would attack German ground positions both days.

American forces were positioned relatively close to the German locations that were targeted by the bombers, so air commanders recommended that the Yanks pull back to allow a margin of safety of 3,000 yards between friendly forces and the areas where bombs would fall. General

B-17Gs of the 303rd Bombardment Group, based at Molesworth, plaster a target in German-occupied Europe. *USAAF via National Archives*

Lieutenant General James "Jimmy" Doolittle, the Commanding General of the Eighth Air Force, confers with Britain's Princess Elizabeth on July 6, 1944. She was visiting the Yanks on that date to officially christen the Seattle-built Block 55 B-17G, tail number 42-102547, as the *Rose of York*. The aircraft was assigned to the 367th Bombardment Squadron of the 306th Bombardment Group, based at Thurleigh, although some sources state that the christening took place at Molesworth. Elizabeth, her father, King George VI, and the whole royal family made several visits to Eighth Air Force fields during the summer of 1944. Elizabeth succeeded her father to the throne nine years later and reigned into the twenty-first century as Queen Elizabeth II. The *Rose of York* completed nearly 100 missions but was shot down over Berlin with BBC correspondent Guy Byum aboard. According to Sergeant Ed Gregory, the crew chief for the *Rose of York*, the bomber was originally named *Princess Elizabeth*, but the name was changed at the insistence of the King. The white rose of York is the symbol of the House of York and of Yorkshire. During the civil wars of the fifteenth century, the white rose was the symbol of York, the rival to the House of Lancaster, whose emblem was the red rose. The conflicts were therefore called the Wars of the Roses. *USAAF via National Archives*

Omar Bradley, commander of the U.S. First Army and overall commander for Cobra, insisted on not pulling back more than 1,000 yards, but a compromise of 1,450 yards for the heavy bombers was finally reached.

The SHAEF weather prognosticators predicted that the haze and ground fog present during the weekend would lift by Monday, July 24, so Operation Cobra was put on the schedule for that afternoon. Over fifteen hundred bombers took off, but as they reached the target area, the majority found their assigned drop zones obscured by clouds and fog, so they aborted on their own initiative. Bradley made the decision to suspend Cobra, but there was a great deal of confusion on the ground when some units did not get the message.

More than a quarter of the bombers, however, arrived over their targets with sufficient visibility to release their bombs. Of the 909 Flying Fortresses launched, 343 bombed the area around Periers and Saint-Lôô, and 35 bombed the Granville railroad junction. Meanwhile, bombers tasked with hitting enemy positions near the front missed due to the fog and killed 150 men of the 30th Infantry Division in a disastrous friendly-fire tragedy that cast a dark shadow over the ultimate success of Operation Cobra.

Bradley might have canceled Cobra altogether, but he chose to launch the following day. On July 25, 1,581 bombers—including 917 B-17s—and five hundred fighters were sent to conduct a saturation bombing campaign across the Marigny-Saint-Gilles region west of Saint-Lô. Of those bombers, 843 Flying Fortresses successfully attacked their targets.

Unfortunately, just as on July 24, the aerial bombardment was marred by a terrible friendly-fire incident. A

A 381st Bombardment Group crew poses at parade rest with its B-17G Flying Fortress at the base near Ridgewell in 1944. *USAAF via National Archives*

pathfinder inadvertently released his ordnance too soon and several dozen bombers followed suit. It could have been much worse, but it was bad enough. Nearly 500 men were wounded, and 111 lost their lives. Among them was Lieutenant General Lesley McNair, who had left a desk job in Washington to travel to the front. He was the highest-ranking U.S. Army officer to be killed in action during World War II, and he died by friendly fire.

As a result of the tragic incidents two days in a row, Eisenhower decided to forbid the use of heavy bombers as tactical weapons near American ground troops for the remainder of the European campaign. On August 8, however, 681 B-17s were tasked with strikes against German troop concentrations opposite British forces near Caen. Again, a friendly-fire incident marred the operation, as twenty-five Canadian soldiers were killed.

Despite the mishaps, the two July days of bombing were devastating for the enemy. July 24 had been bad for the Germans, but July 25 was horrible for them. Though the Allies would not know it until later, the bombing had wiped out approximately a third of German front-line troops in the area. Operation Cobra began sixty days of the most spectacular advance in the history of the U.S. Army.*

THE FIFTEENTH AIR FORCE AND THE MEDITERRANEAN THEATER IN LATE 1944

The Operation Overlord invasion of Normandy in northern France came on June 6, the day after the U.S. Fifth Army marched into Rome. That same week, the Fifteenth Air Force began flying Operation Frantic shuttle-bombing missions that involved attacking eastern Germany and Poland, and then continuing eastward to the Soviet Union rather than returning to Italy. The first Operation Frantic mission involved 130 B-17s, escorted by seventy P-51s, that took off from Italy on June 2. Under command of Lieutenant General Ira Eaker, the bombers struck the marshaling yard at Debreczen in Hungary and landed at Poltava and Mirgorod in the Soviet Union. On June 6, they struck the airfield at Galati in Romania and returned to Soviet bases. Five days later, they departed from the Soviet shuttle bases, bombing the Luftwaffe base at Focsani in Romania before returning to Italy.

In the meantime, more routine Fifteenth Air Force operations continued. On June 4, 550 or more B-17s and B-24s struck communications centers in northwest Italy and on both sides of the Franco-Italian frontier. The next day, as Rome fell to the Allies, more than 440 B-17s and

A B-17G assigned to Lockbourne Army Airfield in Ohio is pictured on September 9, 1944, during a training exercise at the Childress Army Airfield bombing range in Texas. *USAAF via National Archives*

B-24s were launched on missions, with the B-17s bombing railroad bridges at Pioppi and Vado. On June 6, as Operation Overlord was occurring in Normandy, B-17s that were part of a 570-plane package bombed the Belgrade marshaling yard and the Turnu-Severin canal installations, also in Yugoslavia.

On June 7, a mixed force of 340 B-17s and B-24s bombed the dock and harbor installations in the Italian western port city of Livorno, the Voltri shipyards, the Savona railroad junction, and the Vado Ligure marshaling yard. The next day, just 52 B-17s hit the navy yard and dry docks at Pula, Yugoslavia.

On June 9, with approximately 500 B-17s and B-24s airborne, it was back across the Alps for elements of the Fifteenth Air Force, among which were B-17s bombing the industrial area at Munich. The next day, 550 or more heavy bombers were launched over Italy, with B-17s bombing the marshaling yard at Mestre and an oil storage and marshaling yard at Porto Marghera. June 11 saw a similar armada strike targets in Romania and Yugoslavia, with the B-17s attacking Smederevo in Yugoslavia. On June 13, 560 or more B-17s and B-24s went north, and the B-17s targeted aircraft component factories near Munich. The next day, 660 B-17s and B-24s went north again, with the B-17s targeting oil refineries in Budapest.

Oil production was moved to the top of the strategic target list, and B-17s struck the Kragan and Floridsdorf oil refineries near Vienna as part of a six-hundred-plane effort

*For more information on Operation Cobra, see *The Great Offensive: Operation Cobra and the 60 Days That Changed the Course of World War II*, by Bill Yenne.

Chow-hound was a Block 15 Seattle-built B-17G assigned to the 322nd Bombardment Squadron of the 91st Bombardment Group based at Bassingbourn. Originally piloted by Lieutenant Jerry Newquist, it was later flown by Lieutenant Jack Thompson. Lost over France in August 1944, *Chow-hound* was later memorialized as a Revell/Monogram model kit.
USAAF via National Archives

With most of its starboard wing blown off by German flak, a B-17F goes down over Eastern Europe. *USAAF via National Archives*

A bomber stream of B-17Gs of the 2nd Bombardment Group crosses the Alps from the base at Amendola, Italy, headed north to attack Munich, the capital of Bavaria. *USAAF via National Archives*

The tail gunner of a B-17G snapped this picture of a similar aircraft as a large formation of Fifteenth Air Force heavy bombers—including B-24 Liberators and Flying Fortresses—made its way toward the Vienna area for a massive attack. The bombers hit an aircraft factory at Schwechat; the marshaling yard at Vienna/Floridsdorf; and the oil refineries at Korneuburg, Lobau, Moosbierbaum, Schwechat, Vienna/Floridsdorf, and Winterhafen. An estimated thirty Fifteenth Air Force aircraft went down, but the Yanks claimed sixty or more Luftwaffe fighters. *USAAF via National Archives*

on June 16. Five consecutive days of bad weather forced mission cancellations, but a six-hundred-plane contingent was back in action on June 22 over Italy, with B-17s bombing marshaling yards at Fornova di Taro, Modena, and Parma. June 23 saw a resumption of the oil supply campaign, as four hundred B-17s and B-24s struck targets in and around Ploesti. The next day, 335 bombers bombed targets in Romania, including the railroad bridge at Piatra.

On June 25, the attention of the Fifteenth Air Force turned to France, with 650 heavy bombers hitting the marshaling yard and oil installations around Sete. The next day, 677 B-17s and B-24s targeted oil and rail facilities around Vienna. On June 27, approximately three hundred bombers attacked targets in Hungary, Poland, and Yugoslavia, and the B-17s singled out the marshaling yards at Budapest. On the last day of the month, most of the bombers launched were forced to abort because of bad weather, but 188 B-17s and B-24s did hit targets of opportunity across Hungary and Yugoslavia, including Banjaluka, Budapest, Kaposvar, Osztopan, Split, Brac Island, and Zagreb.

The second of July saw 620 bombers again go after targets in Hungary and Yugoslavia. For the B-17s, it was the industrial area at Gyor, a railroad bridge at Szolnok, and marshaling yards at Brod. The next day, both Romania and Yugoslavia were on a target list that included oil facilities and railyards at Arad, Belgrade, Bucharest, Giurgiu, Piatra, Szeged, Timisoara, and Turnu-Severin. On the Fourth of July, 250 or more bombers went into Romania, and the B-17s targeted an oil refinery at Brasov. The next day, 500 bombers went west to France, and the B-17s hit the Montpellier marshaling yards.

On July 6, about 530 B-17s and B-24s in Italy attacked targets such as the Aviano fuel depot area, the Avisio viaduct, the Bergamo steel works, the Porto Marghera oil facility, the Tagliamento-Casarsa della Delizia railroad bridge, an oil refinery at Trieste, and the Verona marshaling yard. The following day, approximately 560 bombers struck in Germany and Yugoslavia, and the B-17s hit two synthetic oil plants at Blechhammer, Germany. On July 8, the targets for 520 or more B-17s and B-24s were in the vicinity of Vienna.

Keeping to the petroleum theme, on July 9, 222 B-17s and B-24s struck the Concordia Vega and Xenia oil refineries at Ploesti. The weekend period of July 14–16 also saw major oil industry attacks, including a 430-plane raid with four refineries at Budapest and Petfurdo on the target list and a 600-plane raid targeting four refineries at Ploesti and the Teleajenul pumping station. There was also a 380-plane effort against oil and aircraft targets around Vienna and the Winterhafen oil depot.

A myriad of tiny European farm fields makes a curious backdrop for this photo of a USAAF B-17G. *USAAF via National Archives*

On July 21, targets in Czechoslovakia took the wrath of 362 B-17s and B-24s, including the Brux synthetic oil refinery. In the latter part of the month, three additional raids on July 22, 28, and 31 targeted Ploesti with an average of 388 heavy bombers.

In the meantime, a 581-bomber attack on July 13 saw B-17s at work within Italy, bombing the marshaling yards at Mestre and railroad bridges at Latisana, Pinzano al Tagliamento, and Venzone. On July 18–20, 200, 400, and 450 B-24s and B-17s, respectively, crossed the Alps to strike targets in Germany that included Memmingen Airfield, the Dornier aircraft works at Manzell, and an aircraft factory at Friedrichshafen.

On July 24, two hundred or more heavy bombers were launched, and the B-17s struck tank repair and ball bearing works in Turin. The next day, 420 B-17s and B-24s struck the Hermann Goering tank works in Linz, Austria (Hitler's hometown), as well as the Villach marshaling yard and targets of opportunity in Austria and Yugoslavia. Two days later, 330 or more B-17s and B-24s went back to Austria to strike the Wiener Neudorf aircraft factory, as well as targets in Bad Voslau, Markersdorf, Thalerhof, and Zwolfaxing. Some bombers also hit the Luftwaffe base at Szombathely in Hungary and oil storage at Berat, Albania. July 27 saw 366 B-17s and B-24s return to Hungary.

The Fifteenth Air Force rounded out the month with a three-hundred-plane effort on July 30 during which the B-17s hit the aircraft factory at Budapest and marshaling yards at Brod in Yugoslavia, followed by a Ploesti mission on July 31.

During August, southern France would figure prominently on the Fifteenth Air Force target list, as the Allies prepared for Operation Dragoon—the invasion of the area that would take place on August 15. The month began with a 330-bomber effort on the second that sent B-17s bombing targets in France, including Le Pouzin oil storage, Portes-les-Valences torpedo factory and marshaling yard, Le Pontet oil storage, and Avignon railroad bridges. The next day, more than 600 bombers crossed the Alps to bomb targets in Germany, including chemical works, fabric works, and two aircraft factories near Friedrichshafen.

On August 6, nearly seven hundred B-17s and B-24s returned to France, bombing numerous targets from oil storage at Le Pontet and Lyon to the railroad bridges at Le Pouzin, Avignon, Tarascon, Rambert, and Givors, as well as marshaling yards at Portes-les-Valences and Miramas, and the U-boat pens at Toulon.

The next day, petroleum was back on the target list as 353 B-17s and B-24s struck synthetic oil refineries at Blechhammer. On August 9, approximately four hundred bombers went out, including B-17s targeting an aircraft assembly plant and a rolling stock plant at Gyor, Hungary, and the marshaling yard and oil refinery at Brod in Yugoslavia. The big oil center at Ploesti would be targeted by an average of three hundred Fifteenth Air Force heavy bombers a half dozen times between August 10 and 19.

August 12 was a busy day for B-17s in the Mediterranean Theater—attacks took place on German gun positions near Savona, Italy, as well as other shuttle-bombing missions. The Eighth Air Force Flying Fortresses had flown from the United Kingdom to the

A large formation of Fifteenth Air Force B-17Gs over the Mediterranean, possibly en route to a target in the Balkans. *USAAF via National Archives*

A top gunner's view of Fifteenth Air Force B-17Gs headed north for a strike against Munich. *USAAF via National Archives*

Contrails billow from the supercharged engines of Fifteenth Air Force Flying Fortresses at high altitude. For the Germans on the ground, the contrails were a sight to be feared, but for the Luftwaffe interceptor pilots, they were a beacon. *USAAF via National Archives*

Soviet Union and then to Fifteenth Air Force bases in Italy. On August 12, seventy-two of the B-17s left Italy for Britain, bombing the Luftwaffe base at Toulouse on the way. Operation Frantic wound down in mid-September as the last shuttling Eighth Air Force B-17s passed through Italy on their way back to the United Kingdom.

Beginning on August 13, the Fifteenth Air Force worked for three days in support of Operation Dragoon. On the first day, about 500 B-17s and B-24s struck gun positions around Genoa, Toulon, and Sete, as well as bridges at Pont-Saint-Esprit, Avignon, Orange, and Crest in France. The next day, 540 B-17s and B-24s returned to Toulon and Genoa. On the third day, as the Operation Dragoon forces prepared to land in France, the Fifteenth Air Force launched its first massed nighttime raid. It involved 252 B-17s and B-24s that took off before dawn and bombed the invasion beaches in the Cannes-Toulon area. Another 28 fighter-escorted B-17s struck highway bridges over the Rhone River.

On August 16, the day after Dragoon, 108 B-17s bombed railroad bridges at Grenoble, Isere-Valence, Saint-Pierre-d'Albigny, and Saint-Vallier.

On August 20, after four straight days of Ploesti raids, 460 or more B-24s and B-17s struck the airfield and marshaling yard at Szolnok, Hungary, as well as oil refineries at Dubova in Czechoslovakia and Zonechowice in Poland. Two days later, approximately 530 B-17s and B-24s bombed targets north of the Alps, and the B-17s concen-trated on oil refineries at Odertal, Germany. On August 23, 472 B-24s and B-17s struck the industrial area south of Vienna and other targets.

The next day, 530 or more B-17s and B-24s struck three oil refineries at Kolin and Pardubice in Czechoslovakia, the marshaling yard at Vinkovci in Yugoslavia, Szeged in Hungary, and other targets. On August 25, 300 B-17s and B-24s targeted Czechoslovakia, specifically aircraft facto-ries at Brno and Kurim, and air bases at Brno and Prostejov. On August 26, 470 or more bombers struck tar-gets in Italy and Romania, and the B-17s homed in on viaducts and bridges at Venzone, Avisio, and Latisana.

The Fifteenth Air Force sent 530 bombers out on August 27, with the B-17s bombing an oil refinery in Blechhammer. The following day, 560 or more bombers attacked targets in Austria, Hungary, and Italy, and the B-17s focused on the Moosbierbaum oil refinery and adja-cent chemical works in Austria. On August 29, 550 heavy bombers spread their wings over targets in Italy, Czechoslovakia, Hungary, and Yugoslavia. August 30 was a lighter day, with only about 100 B-24s and B-17s flying against targets in Yugoslavia. The B-17s struck railroad bridges at Novi Sad and Vranjeco.

August 31 marked the beginning of Operation Reunion. As Soviet forces began to occupy eastern Europe, Fifteenth Air Force heavy bombers flew in to evacuate USAAF air crewmen who were being liberated from German stalags. On the first day of Operation Reunion, thirty-six B-17s flew the freed Americans from Bucharest to Bari in Italy. The next day, sixteen B-17s continued fly-ing men out of Romania.

The Fifteenth Air Force also kept up the bombing oper-ations, opening September with 480 or more B-17s and B-24s attacking targets in Italy, Hungary, and Yugoslavia, including Boara Pisani, Kraljevo, Mitrovica, Moravac, Nish, Novi Sad, and Tesica. On September 3 and 5, an aver-age of over 365 B-17s and B-24s bombed the principal breakout avenues used by German troops retreating from the Balkans. These included rail communications and sup-ply lines south of Budapest, three bridges in the Belgrade area, bridges at Szajol and Szeged in Hungary, railroad bridges at Szolnok and Szob, and the ferry docks at Smederovo, Yugoslavia.

On September 4, meanwhile, almost four hundred B-17s and B-24s assaulted Genoa harbor and bombed communi-cations in northern Italy, including the Avisio viaduct, marshaling yards at Trento, Bronzola, and Ora, and railroad bridges at Ora, Casarsa della Delizia, and Latisana.

With its port wing completely severed, this Flying Fortress cartwheels toward the ground. At this point, it would have been nearly impossible for crewmen to bail out. *USAAF via National Archives*

Occasionally, USAAF B-17s made emergency landings within German-held territory. The Luftwaffe was able to repair at least seven of these bombers and return them to flight status. Painted in German markings, they were used for transport work and clandestine air drops behind Soviet lines. The Luftwaffe also reportedly retained American markings on some captured Forts and used these to infiltrate American bomber formations. *Roger Beseker collection*

On September 7, the action swung back to the retreating Germans in Yugoslavia, as 354 B-17s and B-24s bombed railroad bridges at Brod and Belgrade, and the marshaling yards at Sarajevo and Nish.

Beginning on September 10, the Fifteenth Air Force would be back on the strategic mission for more than a week. That day, 344 B-17s and B-24s struck five ordnance depots and the southeastern industrial area in Vienna, and two oil refineries in the area. On September 12, nearly 330 B-17s and B-24s crossed the Alps to strike the Lechfeld Luftwaffe base and aircraft factories near Munich and Wasserburg. The next day, 350 or more fighter-escorted B-17s and B-24s struck targets in Czechoslovakia, Germany, Italy, and Poland, and the B-17s focused on the oil refinery at Blechhammer. On September 15, an armada of 276 B-17s and B-24s struck Eleusis, Kalamaki, Salamis, and Tatoi in Greece.

On September 17, 440 or more B-17s and B-24s hit four marshaling yards and two oil refineries near Budapest, Germany's last major nonsynthetic oil facility. More tactical than strategic, the idea of the latter mission was to aid the Soviets by hitting the crossroads of Germany's rail network in the area. The mission continued the following day

The Royal Air Force Fortress Mk.IIA was the equivalent of the USAAF B-17E. Most Forts delivered to Britain for use by coastal command had the standard plexiglass nose of the USAAF equivalent aircraft, but this single aircraft was equipped with a special mount containing a Vickers S-type 40mm gun. The idea was to use this weapon to attack surfaced U-boats. The bombardier's station was beneath the gun mount (note the window on the side). *Boeing*

B-17Gs of the Fifteenth Air Force 2nd Bombardment Group attack the railroad yards at Subotica in September 1944. Then part of German-occupied Yugoslavia, Subotica is the second-largest city in the Vojvodina region of Serbia. *USAAF via National Archives*

as 463 B-17s and B-24s bombed railroad facilities in Budapest, Szob, and Szeged in Hungary, and railroad bridges at Novi Sad, Subotica, and Belgrade in Yugoslavia. The next day, 100 Eighth Air Force B-17s passed through Italy after bombing the marshaling yard at Szolnok, Hungary, from bases in the Soviet Union.

On September 21 and 22, an average force of over 420 B-17s and B-24s targeted Hungary, Yugoslavia, and Czechoslovakia, specifically the Malacky Luftwaffe base, the Bratislava petrochemical sector, and transportation targets at Bekescsaba, Brod, Baja, Budapest, Debreczen, Gyor, Hatvan, Kiskore, Novi Sad, and Tiszafured. On September 23, 366 B-24s and B-17s crossed the Alps to strike the industrial area northeast of Munich and the Riem Luftwaffe base. The next day, 147 B-17s attacked

This dramatic photograph amid the contrails of a USAAF bomber stream was taken by a Flying Fortress bombardier. *USAAF via National Archives*

The 99th Bombardment Group B-17s attack the Szob railroad yards near Budapest, Hungary. To aid the Soviet ground advance into German-occupied Hungary, the Fifteenth Air Force attacked the rail network in the area around Budapest several times during the third week of September 1944. *USAAF via National Archives*

the synthetic oil center at Brux in Czechoslovakia and the marshaling yard at Wels in Austria.

October began with a 327-bomber strike on the fourth against Munich and a 400-bomber effort against fifty miles of rail line across Brenner Pass between Italy and Austria. Other targets in Italy included Aviano, Avisio Pinzano al Tagliamento, Casarsa della Delizia, Latisana, Mezzocorona, Ora, Pordenone, and San Dona di Piave. On October 7, more than 350 B-17s and B-24s went north to Austria, targeting the Lobau and Schwechat oil refineries and the Winterhafen oil depot in the Vienna area, as well as other targets of opportunity in Hungary, including marshaling yards at Szombathely and Zalaegerszeg.

On October 10, weather grounded three quarters of the Fifteenth Air Force bomber armada scheduled to work that day, but almost 170 B-17s and B-24s struck four marshaling yards at Treviso and Mestre and bridges at Susegana and San Dona di Piave, plus rail lines in surrounding areas. The following day, about 180 B-17s and B-24s crossed to Austria, bombing targets at Enzesfeld, Graz, Hirtenberg, Vienna, and Zeltweg, as well as the Dravograd, Yugoslavia, railroad bridge on the border with Hungary.

After the friendly-fire incidents that marred heavy bomber support of Operation Cobra, such air support missions were avoided in France, but in Italy, tactical missions took center stage on October 12. On that day, the Fifteenth Air Force flew in support of the U.S. Fifth Army. American troops were advancing out of the Apennines, knowing that if they could enter the Po

Valley before winter it would force the German armies in Italy into a corner.

The final phase of the Fifth Army assault began on October 10, with the 85th Division leading the primary attack against Monte delle Formiche in the center, while the 91st and 88th Divisions maintained pressure on the enemy's flanks. Overhead, fighter bombers, medium bombers, and heavy bombers conducted the series of air strikes known as Operation Pancake. Approximately seven hundred B-17s and B-24s with fighter support bombed ammunition and fuel depots, bivouac areas, vehicle repair shops, a munitions factory, and targets of opportunity in the Bologna area. The 85th Division captured Monte delle Formiche, and on October 13, the 91st Division outflanked the Livergnano Escarpment, forcing the Axis units in the area into a retreat. Six months later, during the second and third week of April 1945, the Fifteenth would undertake another massive ground support campaign in Italy.

Also on October 13, more than 650 B-17s and B-24s struck oil refineries at Blechhammer in Germany and at Floridsdorf, near Vienna. On the target list for the day were motor works, locomotive shops, and marshaling yards at Vienna and Graz, as well as Banhida, Szekesfehervar, and Papa in Hungary, and Hranice and Mezirici in Czechoslovakia.

Scratches on this wartime negative blur with contrails silhouetted against the dark blue winter sky. Two streams of Fifteenth Air Force Flying Fortresses cross paths high over Regensberg on November 4, 1944. On that date, targets north of the Alps for the Fifteenth Air Force included oil storage at Regensburg, the marshaling yards at both Munich and Augsburg, as well as the Reichsbahn yard and a petrochemical facility at Linz. *USAAF via National Archives*

A B-17F, with its number two engine out, is pursued by a Luftwaffe Bf.109 somewhere over the Reich. As the German pilot closes for the kill, it will be the tail gunner's job to see that this doesn't happen. *Author collection*

The nemesis of the Flying Fortress was the Messerschmitt Bf.109, the most widely used Luftwaffe fighter aircraft. It was armed with a cannon that fired through the propeller spiller, plus two machine guns atop the forward fuselage. Many, including the Bf.109G-6 "Gustav" seen here, also carried an additional pair of machine guns in underwing mounts. *Author collection*

With its starboard wing engulfed in a ball of fire, a B-17F Flying Fortress goes down over an enemy railyard. *USAAF via National Archives*

The next day, 317 B-17s and B-24s returned to Blechhammer and proceeded to bomb Odertal. Also bombed that day were marshaling yards at Bratislava in Czechoslovakia, and Hungarian targets at Borzavar, Komarom, Novéé Zaámky, and Ugod. On October 16, around six hundred B-17s and B-24s bombed targets in Austria, including a tank factory and an aircraft engine plant at Steyr, a petrochemical plant, and an ordnance depot at Linz. Alternate targets, both in Austria and Czechoslovakia, included Brux, Graz, Klagenfurt, Neudorf, Pilsen, Salzburg, Sankt Veit, Trieben, and Villach.

On October 17, over 330 heavy bombers returned to the oil and industrial targets at both Blechhammer and Vienna, and hit transportation targets in Austria, Hungary, and Yugoslavia at Banhida, Furstenfeld, Graz, Maribor, Nagykanizsa, and Szombathely. On October 20, more than 480 B-17s and B-24s flew throughout the theater to attack targets such as ordnance works at Milan, an oil refinery at Brux, petroleum storage at Regensburg, the Luftwaffe base at Bad Aibling, and marshaling yards at Rosenheim and Innsbruck.

On October 23, approximately five hundred B-24s and B-17s were tasked to attack a wide variety of targets from a diesel engine factory at Augsburg to Italian bridges in the vicinities of Casarsa della Delizia, Pordenone, Santo Stino di Livenza, and Maniago. Other targets included the Skoda armament works at Pilsen, Czechoslovakia, and German targets such as a marshaling yard at Rosenheim,

the industrial area at Plauen, an aircraft engine plant at Munich, and oil storage depot at Regensburg.

For the remainder of the month, weather limited operations. On October 25, only three B-17s struck a Klagenfurt aircraft factory and the Sankt Veit marshaling yard, and the next day, just seven B-17s struck Innsbruck. On October 28, ten B-17s reached Klagenfurt and eight Flying Fortresses struck Munich.

On the first of November, another major effort was launched by the Fifteenth Air Force, with more than 320 B-17s and B-24s hitting Austrian targets, including factories and rail targets at Vienna, Graz, and Kapfenberg, and targets of opportunity at Ljubljana and Cakove in Yugoslavia and elsewhere in Germany and Hungary. The next day, the weather closed in again and just seven B-17s reached Austrian targets. November 3 was little improved, but forty-six B-17s and B-24s did reach targets around Munich and Vienna.

A huge effort was launched on November 4, involving 715 B-17s and B-24s fanning out across southern Europe to hit petroleum and rail network targets at Augsburg, Erding, Kufstein, Linz, Wels, Muhldorf, Munich, Regensburg, and Rosenheim. Also bombed were German troops at Podgorica, Yugoslavia. The next day, 500 B-24s and B-17s struck the Floridsdorf oil refinery at Vienna in the biggest Fifteenth Air Force assault against a single target during the war.

On November 6, over 580 B-17s and B-24s were launched against targets in Austria from Graz to Vienna, as well as the railroad power substation at Bolzano, just across Brenner Pass from Austria. The next day, over 550 B-17s and B-24s again attacked the Brenner Pass rail line, including bridges south of the pass at Albes, Casarsa della Delizia, Mezzocorona, Ora, and Pinzano al Tagliamento. Also on the target list were locations in Vienna and railroads and troop concentrations in Yugoslavia at Alipasin Most, Maribor, Mitrovica, Novi Pazar, Prijepolje, and Sjenica.

On November 11, after several days of bad weather, 220 or more B-17s and B-24s attacked rail and highway targets in Austria and Germany at Linz, Rosenheim, Salzburg, Villach, Wurzen Pass, and Zell am See, and in Italy at Casarsa della Delizia, Latisana, and Pinzano al Tagliamento. On November 13, just 14 B-17s and B-24s bombed the oil refinery at Blechhammer in a nighttime attack, although five other bombers hit alternate targets in Germany, Poland, and Czechoslovakia. Two days later, eighty heavy bombers struck the benzene industrial solvent plant at Linz, a marshaling yard at Innsbruck, and troop concentrations at Novi Pazar in Yugoslavia, while other bombers diverted to alternate targets.

November 16 again saw 550 or more B-17s and B-24s reach north to Munich and east to Visegrad in Yugoslavia, as well as an alternate target at Innsbruck. The next day, about 630 B-17s and B-24s hit oil refineries at Blechhammer and Vienna, and rail targets at Graz, Gyor, Maribor, Salzburg, Sankt Johann, and Villach. Another maximum effort jumped off on November 18 for the third day in a row, targeting refineries in Vienna and Korneuburg and Luftwaffe bases across Italy at Aviano, Udine, Vicenza, and Villafranca di Verona. The effort continued for a fourth day, with more than 500 B-24s and B-17s concentrating on petroleum industry targets at Linz, Schwechat, Vienna, Vosendorf, and Winterhafen. Petroleum was the theme again on November 20, but only 192 B-24s and B-17s reached primary targets at Blechhammer and Prerov, Czechoslovakia.

Weather would continue to hamper operations through the end of the month. On November 22, only 205 B-17s and B-24s reached Munich, while 214 others had to abort from the primary target because of storm clouds. On November 25, forty heavy bombers flew night missions against Linz, Klagenfurt, Innsbruck, and Munich. Four nights later, 18 B-17s struck the benzene industrial solvent plant at Linz, while three others bombed marshaling yards at Villach, Klagenfurt, and Gmunden.

On December 2, the Fifteenth Air Force was able to launch approximately five hundred B-17s and B-24s against oil refineries at Blechhammer, Odertal, and Vienna, as well as rail targets across central and eastern

The Douglas-built Block 50 B-17G *Kwiturbitchin II* was assigned to the 414th Bombardment Squadron of the 97th Bombardment Group and was based at Amendola, Italy. The "Y" in the triangle identified the group, and the circled numeral "4" was a symbol of the 414th Bombardment Squadron. *USAAF via National Archives*

Europe. The next day, only eighty-five B-24s and B-17s went out, striking the Vienna southeast freight depot, Linz industrial area, and marshaling yards at Innsbruck, Villach, and Klagenfurt.

In the days following, B-17s also dropped supplies to partisans in Yugoslavia, a mission with which they would be tasked in increasing frequency over the coming months.

On December 6, 270 or more B-17s and B-24s were launched, attacking mainly rail targets at Graz in Austria, Bratislava, and Devinska Nova Ves, Czechoslovakia, and the Hungarian towns of Hegyeshalom, Nagycenk, Sopron, Szombathely, and Zalaegerszey. The next day, 31 B-17s and B-24s made predawn attacks on the Salzburg, Klagenfurt, Villach, and Linz marshaling yards. Other targets of the day were communications locations in Wolfsberg, Spittal an der Drau, Mittersill, and Sankt Veit, as well as Trieste. On December 8, 24 B-17s and B-24s returned to targets at Graz, Klagenfurt, Villach, and Vienna.

On December 9, the target list for 170 B-17s and B-24s included Linz and Villach, as well as an oil refinery at Regensburg and factories in Pilsen. The next day, the weather blew in across the Alps, and only 6 B-17s of a 550-plane armada managed to reach Klagenfurt. On December 11, as the weather cleared briefly, the Fifteenth Air Force was able to launch 435 B-17s and B-24s against targets such as the Moosbierbaum oil

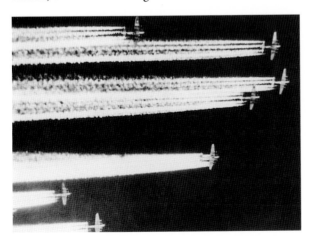

Contrails of an armada of B-17 Flying Fortresses are silhouetted against the dark-blue sky high over Europe. *USAAF via National Archives*

A formation of natural metal B-17Gs assigned to the 533rd Bombardment Squadron of the 381st Bombardment Group heads out across the Essex landscape toward the English Channel for a strike against the Reich. *USAAF via National Archives*

refinery, the Matzleinsdorf railroad station near Vienna, and other targets near Vienna, Tulln, Parndorf, and Graz. On December 12, only 75 B-17s and B-24s went out, striking Blechhammer and Moravska-Ostrava, Czechoslovakia.

A clearing trend in the winter weather began December 15, allowing 330 or more B-17s and B-24s to hit rail network targets at Amstetten, Salzburg, and Innsbruck, as well as Rosenheim, Germany.

December 16 marked the beginning of a five-day push by the Fifteenth Air Force against petroleum targets all across central Europe. On the first day, almost 600 B-24s and B-17s struck a synthetic oil plant at Brux and armament works at Pilsen in Czechoslovakia, as well as the solvent plant at Linz and marshaling yards at Innsbruck and Villach. The next day, 550 or more B-17s and B-24s struck refineries at Blechhammer, Odertal, and Moravska-Ostrava, and marshaling yards at other locations. On December 18, more than 560 B-17s and B-24s returned to Blechhammer, Odertal, and Moravska-Ostrava, and the Floridsdorf refinery at Vienna was added to the list. Additional targets were struck, from Poland to Hungary.

On December 19, 400 B-24s and B-17s were dispatched, hitting Blechhammer and Moravska-Ostrava refineries for the third day in a row. Rail targets at Rosenheim, Strasshof, Villach, Klagenfurt, Graz, Innsbruck, and Sopron were also bombed. The five-day maximum effort against the German oil industry ended the next day with 454 B-17s and B-24s bombing Regensburg and targets in Linz, Salzburg, and Villach.

On Christmas, after several days of downtime, 253 B-17s and B-24s bombed the Brux synthetic oil plant and main marshaling yard at Wels, Austria. Meanwhile, another 145 heavy bombers went after the marshaling yards at Graz, Hall, Innsbruck, Plattling, Rosswein, and Villach. The next day, 380 B-24s and B-17s hit Odertal and Blechhammer for the fourth and sixth time, respectively, during the month. Also on the list on December 26 was the oil refinery at Auschwitz in Poland.

December 27 marked the start of a three-day effort by the Fifteenth Air Force heavy bombers against the Third Reich's rail network in Germany, Austria, and Czechoslovakia, and across Brenner Pass into northern Italy. Indeed, facilities at Brenner Pass would be targeted

A B-17 crew soberly examines the damage that its Flying Fortress incurred on Schkeuditz on August 16, 1944. From left to right the men are Second Lieutenant Fred Kennedy (pilot), Second Lieutenant Zdenek Sedlacek (bombardier), Second Lieutenant Francis Wetherby (co-pilot), and Second Lieutenant David K. Griffiths (navigator). *USAAF via National Archives*

each of the three days. On the first day, more than 520 B-17s and B-24s bombed Bruck an der Mur, Feldbach, Graz, Klagenfurt, Linz, Villach, and Wiener-Neustadt in Austria, as well as Maribor, Yugoslavia, and Venzone, Vipiteno, and Bressanone in Italy.

The next day, 480 or more B-17s and B-24s revisited Bressanone and Venzone and bombed other rail targets at Amstetten, Hieflau, Kallwang, Salzburg, Zwettl, and Kammern, Czechoslovakia. Also targeted were petroleum facilities at Kralupy, Kolin, Pardubice, and Regensburg. On December 29, in the last Fifteenth Air Force assault of 1944, almost 450 B-17s and B-24s struck marshaling yards and other rail facilities at Bressanone, Castelfranco Veneto, Innsbruck, Landshut, Passau, Rosenheim, Salzburg, Udine, and Verona.

Having achieved its planned operational strength of twenty-one heavy bomber groups early in 1944, the Fifteenth Air Force had demonstrated, during the second half of the year, its ability to launch four hundred to five hundred bombers essentially any day it chose. Luftwaffe fighter strength, though declining, was still a problem, but the major impediment had proven to be the turbulent winter weather over the Alps.

The Fifteenth attained a routine during the autumn and early winter of 1944 and would continue to throw armadas of heavy bombers through every hole that appeared in the cloud cover. There was plenty of work left to do in 1945, but the Fifteenth Air Force had the aircraft and crews to meet that challenge.

THE EUROPEAN THEATER OF OPERATIONS AFTER OPERATION COBRA

Although it had devastated German ground forces in Normandy, the use of heavy bombers to support Operation Cobra in July 1944 was marred by friendly-fire incidents that caused the cessation of their use in the ground support role. This permitted the Eighth Air Force to concentrate its strategic bombers on the strategic mission. The full-scale strategic air campaign started in July 1944. The great bulk of the offensive was concentrated on petroleum and transportation, with munitions as secondary targets. The operations of the Eighth, the Fifteenth, and the RAF Bomber Command were then fully coordinated.

In June, the impending capture of the vast refinery complex at Ploesti by the Soviet armies strengthened the case for an all-out attack on the synthetic petroleum industry within Germany, which would then be the Reich's sole source of fuel and lubricants. On June 8, two days after D-day, a new directive stated that the primary strategic aim of the U.S. Strategic Air Forces was to "deny petroleum to enemy armed forces."

After the preliminary attacks on May 12 and 28, the full-scale attack started at the end of June and continued until March 1945. Over one hundred sixty thousand tons of bombs would be dropped during that period on synthetic plants and refineries, and a further twenty-three thousand five hundred tons on petroleum storage depots. There would be 555 separate strikes on 135 different targets, in the course of which every synthetic plant and major refinery known to be in operation was successfully attacked. During the summer, most of the strikes had been made visually.

In July 1944, the requirements of the ground forces also called for strikes against the tank and motor vehicle industries. Attacks on the major producers—from Krupp to Porsche—would be carried out until November 1944.

The first major post-Cobra mission flown by Eighth Air Force B-17s came on July 28, when 652 struck the Leuna synthetic petroleum factory at Merseburg in

A B-17 of the 487th Bombardment Group during the September 10, 1944, raid on a tank factory at Nürnberg (Nuremberg), the ceremonial city of the Nazi Party. The Eighth Air Force launched 385 Flying Fortresses that day, and only three were shot down. *USAAF via National Archives*

B-17s reached south into Alsace and Lorraine, and across the Franco-German border area to hit petroleum sites and bridges at or near Strasbourg, Saarbrucken, and Metz. Another 155 Flying Fortresses bombed bridges at Troyes and Joigny, and 112 hit V-1 sites in the Pas de Calais area. On August 4 and 5, a total of 192 B-17s flew the penultimate Flying Fortress Crossbow missions of the war. The last would involve 107 Flying Fortresses on August 30.

On August 4, it was back to Germany for most B-17 missions, as 231 Flying Fortresses bombed petroleum refineries at Hamburg and Bremen, 221 bombed Peenemunde, 180 bombed Anklam, and 37 hit Nordhof and Einswarden. Meanwhile, 22 bombed Ostend, Belgium, coastal defenses. The next day, 180 B-17s hit Magdeburg, 176 bombed Nienburg, 72 bombed Dollbergen, 157 bombed Luftwaffe bases at Hannover and Helmstedt, and 9 hit targets of opportunity. On August 6, 397 Flying Fortresses plastered Berlin, Brandenburg, and Genshagen, while 16 bombed Luftwaffe bases and 15 bombed targets of opportunity.

Also on August 6, an Operation Frantic shuttle mission put seventy-five B-17s over aircraft factories at Gdynia in Poland. Those bombers and three others continued to fields in the Soviet Union, and the next day, fifty-five of the bombers flew a mission against a petroleum refinery at Trzebina, Poland, at the request of the Red Army. On August 8, the B-17 force hit Luftwaffe

These Flying Fortresses of the 447th Bombardment Group were among eighty-seven Flying Fortresses that bombed the marshaling yards at Koblenz on September 19, 1944. The dashed lines indicate the location of the Reichsbahn yard. An additional thirty-eight B-17s hit other targets in or near Koblenz on the same day. The two rivers are the Rhine and the Moselle, whose confluence is at Koblenz. *USAAF via National Archives*

Germany. Another 36 bombed the Leipzig/Taucha petroleum refinery, 18 bombed the Wiesbaden marshaling yards, and 8 bombed targets of opportunity. The next day, 602 Flying Fortresses bombed targets in and around Merseburg, Gottingen, and Hildesheim. On the last day of the month, Munich and its vicinity were targeted by 650 B-17s.

August began with B-17s back over France. Five Luftwaffe fields and a railway bridge near Orleans and Chartres, south and west of Paris, were hit by 400 B-17s, while the Luftwaffe base at Tours was hit by 76 B-17s. A force of 193 B-17s dropped 2,281 cases of supplies to French resistance partisans in the Savoie and Haute-Savoie region west of Geneva.

On August 2, the Eighth was still isolating the battlefield as 156 B-17s were among a large strike force that attacked petroleum facilities and bridges around Paris, the heart of the transportation hub for northern France. Meanwhile, another 195 B-17s assaulted V-1 missile facilities and rail bridges in northern France. The next day, 345

bases in Romania and continued south to Italy. On August 12, they returned to England, bombing targets around Toulouse on the way.

Meanwhile, on August 7, 112 Eighth Air Force B-17s from England bombed Montbartier and other targets in France. On August 9, 359 Flying Fortresses hit targets along Germany's southwestern border, including Elsenborn, Karlsruhe, Ulm, Spreicher, Saarbrucken, and Luxembourg. That same day, 12 B-17s bombed Eindhoven in the Netherlands, while 16 bombed Aachen, just across the Dutch border in Germany.

August 11 saw a push against rail lines along the Franco-German border that included 152 B-17 sorties against Belfort and Mulhouse. Meanwhile, 275 B-17s struck the extremely well-fortified German positions in and around the French port of Brest ahead of an American ground advance against the city. On August 12, 278 B-17s bombed Luftwaffe bases and rail targets at Buc, Chaumont, Etampes, La Perthe, Metz, and Mondesir. The next day, the Eighth was back to isolating the battlefield as 634 Flying Fortresses hit rail and road targets north of Paris to keep German reinforcements from reaching the front.

Flying Fortresses were in Germany on August 14 when 330 of them struck targets in and around Ludwigshafen and Mannheim. Another wave of 353 B-17s specifically targeted Luftwaffe bases across northern Europe at Chievres, Florennes, Hagenau, Kaiserslautern, Metz, Sindelfingen, Stuttgart, and Trier.

August 15 saw a huge push against Luftwaffe targets with 1,375 Eighth Air Force aircraft and a thousand RAF aircraft involved. The push included 505 Flying Fortresses that hit targets such as Enschede, Frankfurt, Handorf, Köln, Venlo, and Wiesbaden. The following day, the target list included petroleum refineries and aircraft factories, as 588 B-17s targeted Bohlen, Delitzsch, Halberstadt, Halle, Naumburg, Rositz, Schkeuditz, Zeitz, and targets of opportunity.

On August 18, the bombers were mainly back on rail and road targets, as 308 B-17s targeted Bourran, Huy, Liege, Maastricht, Namur, Pacy-sur-Armancon, Tongres, Vise, Yvoir, and targets of opportunity. Meanwhile, 128 bombed the Luftwaffe bases at Eindhoven and Saint-Dizier. August 24's target list included oil and aircraft facilities and Luftwaffe bases within Germany, as 769 Flying Fortresses struck Brux, Freital, Goslar, Kolleda, Leipzig, Merseburg, Nordhausen, Ruhland, Stade, Vorden, Weimar, and targets of opportunity.

This B-17 of the 388th Bombardment Group was one of two dozen Flying Fortresses that plastered the marshalling yards at Darmstadt on September 19, 1944. *USAAF via National Archives*

On August 24, Germany's secret weapons were in the crosshairs as 146 B-17s attacked the Peenemunde research facility, where V-2 ballistic missiles were developed, and 179 hit the Luftwaffe's experimental center at Rechlin. Meanwhile, 169 B-17s bombed the petroleum refinery at Politz, 202 struck Luftwaffe bases at Anklam, Neubrandenburg, and Parow, 31 bombed Henin Littard in France, and 11 bombed targets of opportunity.

Two days later, 174 Flying Fortresses hit petroleum refineries at Gelsenkirchen, 19 bombed the Deelen Luftwaffe base, and 11 bombed targets of opportunity. Meanwhile, another 158 B-17s attacked the fortifications at Brest as ground forces approached. An additional 536 B-17 sorties would be flown against Brest on September 3 and 5.

On August 27, despite heavy cloud cover, 154 B-17 bombardiers managed to attack targets in Denmark and Germany at locations including Ausum, Emden, Esbjerg, Flensburg, and Wilhelmshaven, as well as the islands of Heligoland and Sylt. On August 30, 327 Flying Fortresses hit targets around Bremen, while 282 others went to Kiel for the first attack on U-boat facilities in many months.

September began with all but one of 679 B-17s aborting the mission for the day because of weather. The single plane bombed Hallach, Germany. Three B-17s on a separate mission hit a target in Belgium's Bois de la Haussiere. Two days later, the weather cleared and 325 struck a synthetic petroleum factory at Ludwigshafen. On September 5, 203 Flying Fortresses were over Stuttgart targeting an aircraft engine factory and targets of opportunity, while 277 bombed a synthetic petroleum factory at Ludwigshafen. The same target was revisited on September 7 by 348 B-17s.

Also on September 7, 356 Flying Fortresses attacked an armored vehicle plant near Mainz, a petroleum facility at Kassel, and targets of opportunity. Two days later, 679 B-17s struck the marshaling yard at Mannheim, factories at Dusseldorf, and targets of opportunity, while 68 others dropped supplies to French resistance partisans near Besancon. On September 10, 701 Flying Fortresses bombed factories, Luftwaffe facilities, and targets of opportunity at Furth, Gaggenau, Giebelstadt, Nurnberg, Sindelfingen, and Zuffenhausen.

A Seattle-built Block 90 B-17F of the 95th Bombardment Group unleashes a cluster of five-hundred-pound bombs on a German target. *Courtesy Harry Gann*

The bomber crews referred to escorting fighters as "little friends," but that was a reference only to size. The fighters were an enormous aid to bomber operations and often the difference between life and death. No little friend was a bigger friend to the Eighth Air Force bomber crews than the North American Aviation P-51D Mustang, such as pictured here. The Mustangs were excellent fighters, and their pair of underwing drop tanks gave them the range to escort B-17s all the way to targets deep inside Germany. *USAAF via National Archives*

As Eighth Air Force B-17 Flying Fortresses return to their base in England, the pilots of three escorting fighters roll their P-51D Mustangs overhead in celebration of another successful mission. *USAAF via National Archives*

A formation of 381st Bombardment Group B-17Gs heads into the Reich, circa late November 1944. *USAAF via National Archives*

A three-day maximum effort against the German petroleum industry began the next day. On September 11, refineries and rail facilities were the primary targets as 563 Flying Fortresses attacked Bohlen, Brux, Eisennach, Fulda, Lutzkendorf, Merseburg, Rossla, and Ruhland. Another seventy-five B-17s hit refineries at Chemnitz and continued east to the Soviet Union as part of Operation Frantic.

On September 12, the push against German oil continued as 588 B-17s hit targets in and around Bohlen, Brux, Etterwinden, Fulda, Karlsbad, Kitzingen, Lauta, Magdeburg, Molbis, Plauen, and Ruhland. More than a third bombed the Magdeburg area. The following day, 600 Flying Fortresses bombed refineries and other targets at Altenburg, Darmstadt, Eisenach, Gera, Giessen, Ludwigshafen, Lutzkendorf, Mainz, Merseburg, Stuttgart, and Wiesbaden.

On the ground in eastern Europe, one of the most dramatic events of the war was taking place in German-occupied Warsaw, Poland. With the Soviet armies at the gates of the city, the Polish underground army rose up on August 1 and rebelled against the Germans, hoping the Soviets would enter the city to fight at their side. The Soviets did nothing. Because they planned to subjugate Poland after ejecting the Germans, it was in their interest to let the Poles and Germans kill one another. The partisans managed to capture most of the city, but the Germans counterattacked and the Warsaw uprising devolved into a massacre. The United States wanted to intervene to help the Poles, but the Soviets

On November 26, 1944, three dozen Flying Fortresses targeted the Reichsbahn yards at Bielefeld. They were part of an Eighth Air Force strike package that targeted marshaling yards at Gutersloh, Hamm, and Herford, as well as at Bielefeld. Of the 381 B-17s that were launched, 363 reached their targets and 3 were lost in combat. *USAAF via National Archives*

Two B-17Gs of the 381st Bombardment Group make a low-level dash across the Essex countryside in camouflage war paint. The bomber in the foreground is equipped with the Cheyenne tail turret. Introduced in 1944 on later block B-17Gs from Boeing, Lockheed, and Douglas, the turret was named for the United Air Lines Modification Center at Cheyenne, Wyoming, where most were installed. The Cheyenne turrets afforded better visibility than the earlier turrets, as well as greater gun elevation and a reflector gun sight. Some B-17s were retrofitted with Cheyenne turrets in the field. *USAAF via National Archives*

waited until mid-September to allow the Eighth Air Force to start dropping supplies. On September 15, 110 B-17s finally air-dropped supplies into Warsaw and continued on to the Soviet Union as part of Operation Frantic. Another such mission involving 107 Flying Fortresses was flown on September 18, but the Germans defeated the Poles a few days later, marking an end to Operation Frantic. The last bombers would filter back into England by way of Italy by October 8.

Meanwhile, on September 17, 815 Flying Fortresses attacked more than a hundred antiaircraft sites and a Luftwaffe base in the Netherlands. Two days later, the strategic campaign against Germany continued when 722 B-17s attacked Darmstadt, Dillenburg, Dortmund, Emmerich, Hamm, Koblenz, Limburg, Munster, Osnabruck, Raesfeld, Rheine, Soest, Wesel, Wetzlar, Wiesbaden, and other targets. On September 21, 154 B-17s attacked the synthetic petroleum factory at Ludwigshafen and 141 hit the marshaling yard at Mainz. On September 22, 410 Flying Fortresses attacked the motor vehicle plants at Kassel, while 10 bombed Wetzlar and 7 bombed targets of opportunity.

A concentrated five-day effort against German industry began on September 25, and 400 Flying Fortresses attacked Ludwigshafen and 410 hit Frankfurt. The next day, 383 bombed Osnabruck, 381 bombed Bremen, and 13 hit Bemerhaven, while 18 others bombed Luftwaffe bases and other sites. On September 27, 421 B-17s bombed Köln, 214 bombed the refinery at Ludwigshafen, 171 hit Mainz, 10 attacked Blatzheim, and 4 others bombed targets of opportunity. On September 28, 382 B-17s bombed Magdeburg, 301 hit Marseburg, and 45 bombed targets of opportunity. On the last day of September, 257 B-17s bombed the Bielefeld marshaling yard and 288 hit targets in Munster.

October began with a continuation of the assault on German industry. On October 2, 656 Flying Fortresses attacked facilities in Kassel, 110 struck Köln, and 69 bombed other targets, including Fritzlar Luftwaffe base, Wiesbaden, and Gesecke. The following day, 454 B-17s bombed Nurnburg and 209 hit targets that included Giebelstadt, Köln, Ludwigshafen, Ulm, Ottingen, and Wesseling.

Köln was the target for 243 B-17s on October 5, while 303 hit Luftwaffe bases at Munster and 62 bombed targets at Brechten, Dortmund, Koblenz, and Rheine. The next day, 382 Flying Fortresses bombed targets in the Berlin area, while 442 bombed Freienwalde, Kappeln, Neubrandenburg, Stargard, Stettin, Stralsund, and targets of opportunity. On October 7, many petroleum facilities were hit, as 865 Flying Fortresses bombed targets that included Bielefeld, Bohlen, Dresden, Freiburg, Hameln, Lutzendorf, Merseburg, Nordhausen Luftwaffe base, Politz, Ruhland, and Zwickau.

On October 9, 329 B-17s bombed the ball bearing factories at Schweinfurt for the first time in three months, while 210 hit the marshaling yard at Mainz and 148 attacked the aircraft engine factory near Mainz. Two days later, 57 B-17s struck the Wesseling synthetic petroleum factory while 73 others bombed the Koblenz marshaling yard. On October 12, 267 B-17s attacked factories at Bremen.

Three straight days of action began on October 14, with 847 Flying Fortresses hitting targets in Germany that included Saarbrucken and Kaiserslautern, as well as the Köln area. Over the next two days, 840 B-17 sorties attacked targets in the area between Köln and Koblenz. On October 18, 300 B-17s hit Kassel, while 112 attacked the Köln area again. The next day, more than 500 B-17s hit targets in and around Mannheim, while 82 hit targets of opportunity that included Bad Kreuznach, Karlsruhe, Rudesheim, and Steyer.

On October 22, 352 B-17s attacked Munster, 171 targeted Hannover, 148 bombed Braunschweig, and 35 hit Bielefeld. Three days later, 722 Flying Fortresses plastered petroleum refineries at Hamburg in two waves, while 27 bombed the synthetic petroleum plants at Gelsenkirchen and 100 others bombed the marshaling yard at Hamm. October 26 brought attacks against Bielefeld, Gutersloh, and Munster by 476 B-17s, while 376 hit targets in Hannover. On October 28 and 30, Munster was revisited by 370 Flying Fortress sorties, while 393 sorties targeted the marshaling yard at Hamm.

November operations got under way on the first with another twenty-three B-17s striking the marshaling yard at Hamm, while 113 Flying Fortresses hit a petroleum facility at Gelsenkirchen and 34 bombed Rudesheim and Koblenz. The next day, 593 Flying Fortresses attacked the Leuna synthetic petroleum facility at Merseburg in two waves and 185 others bombed targets, including Halle, Rheine, Sterkrade, and Wolfenbuttel.

The synthetic petroleum industry was the main target again on November 4 for 748 Flying Fortresses bombing targets in Bottrop, Hamburg, Hamm, Neunkirchen, Nordholz, and Saarbrucken. The next day, marshaling yards were hit by 869 B-17s in Frankfurt, Hanau, Kaiserslautern, and Ludwigshafen. On November 6, 283

Bombing through partial cloud cover, B-17Fs of the Eighth Air Force 94th Bombardment Group rain ordnance on German targets. The 94th was based at Bury St. Edmunds from May 1943 through the end of the war. *Courtesy Harry Gann*

This 452nd Bombardment Group B-17G was one of 62 Eighth Air Force Flying Fortresses to bomb the railyard at Giessen on December 4, 1944. Meanwhile, 221 Forts hit the yards at Mainz, the other primary target for the day. Many other bombers diverted to targets of opportunity, especially Friedburg. *USAAF via National Archives*

B-17s bombed refineries in Hamburg, while 101 attacked a refinery in Bottrop and 65 hit a chemical plant at Duisburg. Another 254 attacked targets in Neumunster and 555 bombed the marshaling yards. November 8 saw a smaller air assault than in recent days, with 192 B-17s attacking the petroleum plant at Merseburg. A second wave against the same target aborted because of weather.

On November 9, Eighth Air Force operations shifted to the transportation grid on the Franco-German border that the Germans were using to bring ground forces into the line to oppose the American advance against Germany. Rail targets in and around Metz, Thionville, and Saarbrucken were hit by 695 Flying Fortresses, and 28 bombed Koblenz. The next day, 374 B-17s attacked Luftwaffe bases at or near Köln and Wiesbaden. November 11 saw 193 B-17s bomb rail facilities at Koblenz, Oberlahnstein, and Rheine, while 100 attacked a refinery at Gelsenkirchen.

By mid-November—three weeks after the American Ninth Army captured Aachen, the first city within Germany to be captured by Allied troops—the Germans were pouring large numbers of troops into the line to oppose the First and Ninth Armies as they battled their way eastward. SHAEF asked the Eighth Air Force to work over the German supply lines, and on November 16, 976 Flying Fortresses blasted transportation targets east of Aachen near Duren and Eschweiler.

On December 4, 1944, the Reichsbahn yard at Friedburg was a target of opportunity for 119 Flying Fortresses, including these 487th Bombardment Group B-17Gs. On that date, the Eighth Air Force launched 457 B-17s against the railyards at Mainz and Giessen, but only 283 hit the primary targets. *USAAF via National Archives*

December 12, 1944, saw the Eighth Air Force launch 497 Flying Fortresses against the Reichsbahn yard at Darmstadt. This B-17 was one of 461 to hit the primary target. Of the others, 23 aborted after takeoff, 9 diverted to Dieburg, and 4 bombed a target of opportunity. No Flying Fortresses were shot down in these operations. *USAAF via National Archives*

On November 20, strategic targets were back on the list, and 154 B-17s hit targets at Gelsenkirchen and Munster. The next day, 200 Flying Fortresses bombed the synthetic petroleum plant at Merseburg and 577 attacked rail and other targets at Apolda, Bielefeld, Friedburg, Giessen, Hersfeld, Hunfeld, Koblenz, Leeuwarden Luftwaffe base, Lingen, Meppen, Merseburg, Osnabruck, Quakenbruck, and Wetzlar.

The synthetic fuel facility at Merseburg headed the target list on November 25, receiving the attention of 671 B-17s. The next day, 243 B-17s attacked the petroleum refinery at Misburg, while 366 bombed rail targets at or near Altenbekin, Bielefeld, Gutersloh, Hamm, Herford, and Osnabruck. Both Hamm and Misburg were retargeted on November 28 by a total of 685 Flying Fortress sorties, while Osnabruck was bombed by 36 B-17s. Meanwhile, on November 27, the marshaling yards at Bingen and Offenburg were targeted by 329 B-17s.

On the last day of the month, 417 Flying Fortresses hit the Leuna synthetic petroleum facility at Merseburg in two waves, while 514 B-17s bombed targets that included Bohlen, Fulda, Gera, Gotha, Lutzkendorf, Meerane, Ohrdruf, Rudolstadt, Saalfeld, Weissenfels, and Zeitz.

December 2 saw 125 Flying Fortresses bomb the Oberlahnstein marshaling yard and 9 hit the Lutzel yard at Koblenz. A second, 160-plane B-17 mission against Koblenz aborted because of the weather. Two days later,

400 B-17s attacked the marshaling yards at Kassel and Soest, while a second wave of 283 hit the marshaling yards at Mainz and Giessen. Another 560 bombed targets of opportunity that included Friedburg's marshaling yard, Fulda, and barges on the Rhine River.

On December 5, 404 Flying Fortresses hit factories in Berlin, while 25 attacked targets of opportunity. The following day, 446 B-17s revisited the Leuna facility at Merseburg in two waves, while 54 struck other targets such as Hannover and the town of Merseburg. On December 9, 395 B-17s hit targets across the Reich, including Boblingen, Echterdingen, Halingen, Stuttgart, and Unterturkheim. On December 10, the target was the Lutzel marshaling yard at Koblenz that had been spared by clouds eight days earlier. The second time, 277 B-17s hit the primary target and 13 bombed targets of opportunity.

The following day, the Eighth Air Force launched its largest strategic mission over Germany to date, setting a record that would be surpassed only twice. A total of 1,586 heavy bombers, along with 841 fighters, took off for Germany on December 11. It is a clear measure that the Eighth was a very-well-oiled machine that only 5 bombers and 2 fighters were shot down. Marshaling yards were the principal targets for the Flying Fortress force, and 319 Flying Fortresses hit the one at Frankfurt, 353 the one at Giessen, and 135 the yard at Koblenz. Another 171 of the B-17s bombed bridges around

Mannheim, while 24 others bombed targets of opportunity, including Euskirchen.

To underscore the power of the Eighth Air Force at its apogee, on December 12, 895 bombers and 928 fighters were dispatched toward Germany. Of those, 461 B-17s bombed the marshaling yard at Darmstadt, 337 bombed the Leuna facility at Merseburg, and 30 hit other targets, including Dieburg and Nordhausen. Only a single Flying Fortress was lost over Germany that day, although at least two limped home so badly shot up that they had to be written off. Such was the nature of the durable Flying Fortress that even badly damaged aircraft made it home.

Railroad and industrial targets were on the agenda for December 15, as 318 B-17s bombed Kassel, 327 hit Hannover, and 11 diverted to targets of opportunity. Bad weather on December 16 caused most of the Eighth Air Force strike package to abort, but 89 B-17s managed to reach Stuttgart and 34 bombed targets that included Bietingheim. Weather and visibility over the following days caused most missions to be canceled after takeoff, but on December 18, 219 Flying Fortresses managed to bomb rail targets in Bonn, Kaiserslautern, Koblenz, and Köln.

Meanwhile, on the ground, the Germans had launched a major offensive against American positions on the morning of December 16. Codenamed *Wacht am Rhein* (Watch on the Rhine), the attack by two entire Panzer armies surprised, stunned, and overwhelmed American forces in the mountainous Ardennes region of Belgium. The spectacular gains made by the Germans during the Ardennes offensive created a huge bulge in the territory previously occupied by the Americans, leading to the unfolding battle to be called the "Battle of the Bulge." To cut off the German supply lines that were funneling men and materiel into the Bulge, the Eighth Air Force, including 168 B-17s, spent December 19 working over road and rail junctions across the affected area.

During the following days, blizzard conditions across northern Europe hindered activities on the ground and also precluded Eighth Air Force operations until December 23. On that date, the Eighth was able to send 423 bombers and 636 fighters to attack road and rail chokepoints behind the front. The armada included 246 B-17s that bombed marshaling yards at Ehrang, Homburg, and Kaiserslautern.

On the day before Christmas, a high-pressure front brought a spectacular reversal in the weather, with clear skies all across western Europe. Allied tactical aircraft were able to intervene against Germans in the Bulge, and the Eighth Air Force was able to launch its biggest operation

of the war. The largest strategic air attack in history, it involved 2,034 bombers and 853 fighters of which only 12 bombers and 10 fighters were shot down. The fighters and bombers, in turn, shot down a confirmed ninety-two Luftwaffe aircraft.

In the great Christmas Eve campaign, 1,331 Flying Fortresses operating in two vast waves bombed Luftwaffe facilities at Babenhausen, Darmstadt, Ettinghausen, Frankfurt, Giessen, Gross Ostheim, Haildraum, Kaiserslautern, Koblenz, Merzhausen, Nidda, Pforzheim, and Zellhausen.

Christmas Day saw no respite for the Eighth Air Force, with 156 B-17s hitting rail targets at Ahrweiler, Bad Krueznach, Bad Munster, Eller, Hermeskeil, Kaiserslautern, Marscheid, Simmern, and elsewhere in support of American troops in the Bulge. The next day, as the ground interdiction campaign continued, weather limited Flying Fortress operations to fifty-seven strikes on rail targets in and around Andernach, Neuwied, and Sinzig. Weather continued to be an issue on December 27, but 403 B-17s succeeded in attacking rail targets at Altenahr, Andernach, Bullay, Eckfeld, Euskirchen, Fulda, Gerolstein, Hildesheim, and Neuwied.

An Eighth Air Force Flying Fortress heads home across the English Channel after a mission to Giessen in December 1944. Christmas Eve 1944 saw the largest number of heavy bombers launched in a single day. Only a dozen bombers out of 2,034, and only 10 fighters out of 853, were shot down that day, but one of them was the lead B-17, piloted by the operation's commander, Brigadier General Colonel Frederick Walker Castle. *USAAF via National Archives*

On December 18, 1944, these 452nd Bombardment Group B-17Gs were part of a group of 157 Eighth Air Force Flying Fortresses that unleashed its high-explosive ordnance on the Reichsbahn yard at Mainz, while 13 other B-17s bombed targets of opportunity. Only 1 B-17 in this strike package was lost. *USAAF via National Archives*

The weather was clear at high altitude, but cloud cover obscured some targets across Germany on December 18, 1944. Of the B-17 strike package dispatched to Mainz, most connected with the primary target, but of the 385 Flying Fortresses that were to have attacked the Kalk Reichsbahn yard at Koln, only 32 hit the primary. Among the others, 102 diverted to Koblenz and 74 to Kaiserslautern. *USAAF via National Archives*

The biggest Eighth Air Force armada since Christmas Eve, 1,275 bombers and 606 fighters left England on December 28. Again mainly targeting railroad facilities, 840 B-17s bombed locations at Bruhl, Irlich, Koblenz, Sieburg, Sinzig, and Troisdorf. Among the bridges that were hit that day was the Ludendorf Bridge across the Rhine River at Remagen. Patched up after December bombing attacks, it would be captured by the Americans on March 7—the first intact bridge across the Rhine to be seized, and thereby a key means of funneling American forces into the heart of Germany.

Rail facilities in Germany and Luxembourg continued to dominate the target list on December 29, as 503 Flying Fortresses attacked Aschaffenburg, Bingen, Bullay, Diekirch, Frankfurt, Grosslittgen, and Wittlich. The next day, the Eighth Air Force launched 1,315 bombers and 572 fighters in the continuing war against the rails. Among them, 216 bombed Kaiserslautern and 681 attacked targets in and around Bischoffsheim, Bullay, Kassel, and Mannheim.

On New Year's Eve, the Eighth Air Force was able to put at least part of its armada of 1,327 bombers and 785 fighters back on strategic targets deep within the Reich. Among the targets were refineries and other sites in Hamburg, which were struck by 303 B-17s. Another

181 B-17s attended to targets at Heligoland, Misburg, Nordholz, Stade, and Wenzendorf. Tactical targets addressed by a wave of 492 B-17s included Blumenthal, Ehrang, Koblenz, Krefeld, Monchen-Gladbach, Neuss, Prum, and the bridge at Remagen. The tactical importance of the bridge to ground forces was yet to be realized; it was still seen as a means for the Germans to get men and materiel into the fight, and as such, it needed to be bombed.

As 1944 came to a close, it was evident that the great air offensive that began in late July—and climaxed with the great Christmas Eve operation—was producing its desired impact on the German economy and German industrial output. There was at least a 15 percent loss of armament output in the last half of 1944, compared with a 5 percent decrease for the last half of 1943 and a 10 percent decline during the first half of 1944.

The attacks on the synthetic petroleum industry, which were the top priority during that period, were found to have cost Germany a considerable portion of its methanol and rubber supply, as well as the supply of synthetic nitrogen needed for explosives. Those products were either produced in conjunction with synthetic petroleum or their manufacture required by-products of petroleum production.

A formation of 381st Bombardment Group B-17Gs heads toward the target escorted by a Republic P-47 Thunderbolt fighter. The Thunderbolt's wings are marked with the black-and-white "invasion stripes" that were painted on Allied tactical aircraft during and after Operation Overlord in June 1944. *USAAF via National Archives*

Between July and the end of 1944, synthetic nitrogen output was reduced from over seventy-five thousand tons to twenty thousand tons monthly. The Germans were forced to curtail the use of nitrogen in agriculture and then to cut supplies used for the production of explosives. Methanol production, also necessary for explosives manufacturing, was similarly cut. The shortages were largely responsible for the 20 percent drop in ammunition production in the last half of 1944. By the end of 1944, synthetic rubber production had been reduced to approximately 15 percent of the January-to-April average.

As the raids on the aircraft industry continued from summer into autumn, their center of gravity shifted from assembly plants to engine production. Production was more vulnerable than assembly, owing to the greater difficulty of dispersal and the lack of excess capacity in the industry. Aircraft production in December was only 60 percent of what it had been in July, and the total loss of output for the period, due to both direct and indirect effects of bombing, was about 25 percent.

The attacks on tank production set back the German expansion program and caused a 20 percent loss of output in the latter half of 1944. The attacks on motor vehicle production also caused a 20 percent loss in production but reduced the total stock of trucks and passenger cars by only 4 percent. Motor transport was undoubtedly more limited by the gasoline shortage than by the reduction in the vehicle supply.

Massive attacks on the Ruhr industrial area in the last quarter of 1944 reduced its steel output by 80 percent. Total munitions output reached its peak in July 1944 and fell thereafter. By December, it had declined to 80 percent of the July peak, and it was only through the use of existing supplies of components and raw materials that that level could be maintained. German steel production (including that of the occupied territories) declined from two million tons in September to one million tons in December. Approximately 80 percent of the decline was due to the air strikes.

The offensive against the transportation network, beginning in September 1944, was probably the most important single cause of Germany's ultimate economic collapse. Between August and December, freight car loadings fell by approximately 50 percent.

The great air offensive was the main factor in reducing German industrial output. Without it, production would almost certainly have increased. As 1944 ended, a corner had been turned, but there was still work to be done, and the Eighth Air Force still had hundreds upon hundreds of Flying Fortress sorties to be flown.

New Year's Eve 1944 saw more than 900 Flying Fortresses, including these B-17Gs of the 379th Bombardment Group, launched against targets across Germany. About a third of the B-17s dispatched that day hit targets in and around Hamburg, while 109 bombers targeted Neuss, 83 hit the Krefeld area, and 69 zeroed in on Reichsbahn targets at Ehrang. *USAAF via National Archives*

A B-17G of the 486th Bombardment Group with a Cheyenne tail turret opens its bomb bay over Swinemunde on March 11, 1945. The USAAF was able to blast the railroad facilities in this seaside Pomeranian city with 220 B-24 Liberators and 441 Flying Fortresses on that date. *USAAF via National Archives*

B-17G Flying Fortresses of the Fifteenth Air Force 99th Bombardment Group cross a level landscape, possibly Italy's Po River Valley or the plains of eastern Austria. The Cheyenne tail turret gave gunners much better visibility and field of fire. *USAAF via National Archives*

CHAPTER SIX

B-17 OPERATIONS IN 1945

THE FIFTEENTH AIR FORCE AND THE MEDITERRANEAN THEATER

For several months before the beginning of 1945, the Mediterranean Theater was that in name only. The Axis ceased to operate on or above the Mediterranean Sea, and its ground troops were on the run in both Italy and the Balkans. For the B-17s and other aircraft of the Fifteenth Air Force, targets were more often in Germany and Austria than in any land washed by any part of the Mediterranean. The job of the Fifteenth since autumn 1944 had been to tighten the noose around the Third Reich. Operationally, the key targets were the railroad network and the oil industry. A great deal of impact had been made in 1944, but the job continued into the new year.

The main impediment faced by the Fifteenth Air Force in the final months of 1944 had been the harsh winter weather over the Alps that separated the Fifteenth Air Force bases in Italy from targets within the Reich. Such would continue to be the case in January 1945. Indeed, during the first two weeks of the year, only January 8 permitted operations. On that day, over three hundred B-17s and B-24s struck Austrian railroad yards at Graz, Klagenfurt, Linz,

Salzburg, and Villach. Over the following week, the bombers flew only a handful of reconnaissance missions.

Finally, on January 15, an opening appeared, and more than 400 B-24s and B-17s hit marshaling yards and other railroad communications around Vienna, and the marshaling yard at Treviso in Italy. Another two-day window in the weather came January 19 and 20, and the Fifteenth Air Force launched an average of 375 bombers each day against rail targets in Yugoslavia, Austria, and Germany, and oil storage facilities at Regensburg. Weather hampered operations only over Zagreb. However, attempts to launch further missions were stymied by the weather until the last day of the month, when over 670 B-24s and B-17s were able to hit the Moosbierbaum oil refinery, as well as other targets at Graz, Maribor, and elsewhere.

Before turning nasty again, the clear weather held for the first day of February, allowing over 300 B-17s and B-24s to return to the Moosbierbaum refinery and the marshaling yards at Graz, and to target Furstenfeld and Klagenfurt. The USAAF took advantage of the next clearing on February 5 by launching an armada of 730 or more B-17s and B-24s against oil storage facilities at Regensburg and railyards at

Death and disaster on a cold day in January 1945, as at least one Flying Fortress disintegrates. The burning wing fragment on the right is literally cartwheeling across the sky. Was it an unlucky direct hit by a German 88mm flak battery? There appear to be two B-17 tail assemblies among the fragments, suggesting that it may have been a collision. *USAAF via National Archives*

Rosenheim, Salzburg, Straubing, and Villach. Two days later, the weather again cooperated, and 680 B-17s and B-24s struck oil refineries and other sites at Bratislava, Moosbierbaum, Schwechat, and Vienna, as well as oil storage facilities at Pula and the shipyard and harbor at Trieste. On February 8, more than 500 B-24s and B-17s struck Vienna and Graz, and the following day, a small number of bombers revisited those sites.

A major effort involving 640 B-17s and B-24s went after Vienna and Graz on February 13, and also targeted Maribor, Zagreb, and the Pula harbor. The next day, more than 500 B-24s and B-17s struck the Floridsdorf, Lobau, Moosbierbaum, Lobau, and Schwechat oil refineries in the Vienna area, as well as marshaling yards at Gleisdorf, Graz, Klagenfurt, Maribor, Villach, and Zagreb. Many of the same targets were revisited on February 15 by 650 B-24s and B-17s. The target list also included Wiener-Neustadt and Fiume in Italy.

On February 16, the focus shifted from Austria to Germany and Italy, and about 630 B-24s and B-17s targeted Luftwaffe bases at Landsberg, Neubiberg, and Regensburg, as well as rail targets along the Brenner Pass route north of Bolzano. The next day, 500 B-17s and B-24s returned to Austria to strike the marshaling yard, station, and benzene industrial solvent plant at Linz, as well as targets in Bruck an der Mur, Graz, Sankt Valentin, Steyr, Villach, and Wels. Also on the list for the day—and again on February 20—were the Adriatic seaports of Fiume, Pula, and Trieste.

On February 18, 160 B-17s attacked the industrial solvent plant and the main marshaling yard and station at Linz, Austria. For the next three days, the Fifteenth Air Force averaged five hundred-plane raids each day, mainly against Austrian rail targets at Bruck an der Mur, Graz, Klagenfurt, Schwechat, Vienna, Wiener-Neustadt, and Zeltweg, as well as Sopron, Hungary.

On February 22, the U.S. Strategic Air Forces in Europe undertook Operation Clarion, which specifically targeted communications centers in Germany, Austria, and Italy. The Fifteenth Air Force participation on the opening day of the operation involved more than 350 B-17s and B-24s bombing fifty or more sites. The next day, as the operation continued, about 380 B-17s and B-24s bombed targets at Kitzbuhel, Klagenfurt, Knittelfeld, Villach, and Worgl in Austria, as well as Udine, Italy.

More than 500 B-17s and B-24s were launched on February 24 against rail targets at Ferrara, Graz, Klagenfurt, Padua, Udine, and Verona. The next day, more than 600 B-17s and B-24s struck marshaling yards in Amstetten, Linz, Salzburg, and Villach. On February 27, 540 B-24s and B-17s struck marshaling yards at Augsburg in Germany and Jenbach, Lienz, and Salzburg in Austria.

On the last day of the month, the Fifteenth Air Force sent about 680 B-17s and B-24s against Lienz, but the main targets of the day were in Italy, specifically Albes, Bolzano, Brescia, Bressanone, Brunico, Conegliano, Fortezza, Ora, Verona-Parona di Valpolicella, Vicenza, and Vipiteno.

The first day of March saw a major effort by about 630 B-24s and B-17s against the Moosbierbaum oil refinery, although many bombers hit alternate targets and targets of opportunity, such as rail facilities at Amstetten, Feldbach, Klagenfurt, Knittelfeld, Maribor, Sankt Polten, and Villach. The next day, 470 B-24s and B-17s returned to many of the alternate targets from March 1 and also attacked marshaling yards at Linz and Brescia in Italy.

On March 4, the focus shifted eastward as more than 630 B-17s and B-24s struck marshaling yards at Sopron and Szombathely, Hungary, and Zagreb and Ljubljana in Yugoslavia. In Austria, Graz, Knittelfeld, Sankt Veit, Wiener-Neustadt, and Zeltweg were also targeted. Weather limited operations until March 8, when more than 550 B-17s and B-24s bombed marshaling yards at Hegyeshalom and Komarom, Hungary, and Verona in Italy, as well as the locomotive depot at Maribor and the steel works at Kapfenberg. Two days later, 191 heavy bombers hit the Verona-Parona di Valpolicella railroad bridge.

The three days beginning on March 12 saw a series of maximum-effort missions all across central Europe. On the first day, 790 B-17s and B-24s focused on the Floridsdorf oil refinery at Vienna and hit alternate targets, such as the marshaling yards at Graz, Wiener-Neustadt, and Zeltweg. The next day, 569 B-17s and B-24s struck the marshaling yard at Regensburg, and on the third day, 634 B-17s and B-24s bombed the Szony and Almasfuzito oil refineries, and marshaling yards at Komarom in Hungary, as well as targets in Graz, Knittelfeld, Nové Zámky in Czechoslovakia, Wiener-Neustadt, and Zagreb.

The Fifteenth Air Force's deepest mission into Germany occurred on March 15, when 109 B-17s struck the oil refinery at Ruhland, north of Dresden. Another 103 bombed the alternate target, the refinery at Kolin, Czechoslovakia. Still other bombers hit targets across Austria that day. The following day saw a 720-plane maximum effort against petroleum and oil targets in Austria, specifically at Korneuburg, Schwechat, and Vienna.

A Fifteenth Air Force B-17G opens its bomb bay over the target. *USAAF via National Archives*

A Douglas-built Block 55 B-17G assigned to the 341st Bombardment Squadron, 97th Bombardment Group, drops fragmentation clusters on its target. Such ordnance would have been used by the Fifteenth Air Force against German troop concentrations in Italy and Yugoslavia. *USAAF via National Archives*

On March 19 and 20, two more maximum-effort missions occurred, involving more than 800 and 760 heavy bombers, respectively. The missions targeted rail and petroleum facilities at Altenmarkt an der Alz, Amstetten, Garching an der Alz, Kagran, Klagenfurt, Korneuburg, Lambach, Landshut, Muhldorf, Passau, Plattling, Sankt Polten, Sankt Veit, Steyr, Wels, and Wiener-Neustadt.

Slightly smaller armadas of Fifteenth Air Force bombers sustained a campaign that averaged more than 635 B-17s and B-24s each day for the next six days. The targets were related to petroleum production and rail transportation but also included factories and Luftwaffe bases. The locations in Germany and Austria were Bruck an der Mur, Bruck an der Leitha, Erding, Gmund, Graz, Klagenfurt, Munich, Neuburg an der Donau, Neunkirchen, Plattling, Ruhland, Sankt Polten, Sankt Valentin, Strasshof, Vienna, Villach, Wels, Wiener-Neustadt, and Zeltweg. In Czechoslovakia, the B-17s and B-24s attacked targets at Bratislava, Ceske Budejovice, Cheb, Kralupy, Neratovice, Prague, and Vltava. Additional targets during the huge air offensive of March 21–27 included Szombathely in Hungary, Udine in Italy, and Pragersko in Yugoslavia.

On March 30, only about 60 B-17s and B-24s went out, striking rail facilities at Graz, Klagenfut, and Vienna. The month ended with 540 B-17s and B-24s

Having limped to a safe landing, this Flying Fortress was the subject of the attention of onlookers. The damage may have been from flak, or this may have been one of a number of B-17s to survive having been rammed by a Luftwaffe fighter. The "Y" in the circle denotes the Fifteenth Air Force 2nd Bombardment Group, while the horizontal line with the three hash marks is the symbol of the 429th Bombardment Squadron. *USAAF via National Archives*

targeting the railyards at Linz and Villach in Austria and Treviso, Italy, on March 31.

April would be the last full month of Fifteenth Air Force offensive operations during World War II, but among the missions flown would be some of the largest, including two in which more than eight hundred heavy bombers were involved.

The month began with almost 400 B-24s and B-17s launched against rail targets at such familiar locations as Graz, Maribor, Sankt Polten, Selzthal, Villach, and Zeltweg. On April 2, almost 600 B-24s and B-17s hit the marshaling yards at Graz, Krems, and Sankt Polten, and a railroad bridge on the Sulm River. On April 5, 457 B-24s and B-17s struck a railroad bridge at Dravograd, Yugoslavia, the marshaling yards and locomotive depots at Brescia, Alessandria, and Turin, as well as the Luftwaffe base at Udine.

On April 6, the Fifteenth Air Force focused on targets within Italy, sending 387 B-17s and B-24s against marshaling yard antiaircraft gun positions and an ordnance depot at Verona, and the marshaling yard and a small arms plant at Brescia. The next day, 128 B-17s and B-24s struck the Mezzocorona railroad bridge, a nearby road bridge, and a railroad bridge near Verona. Also included in the April 7 target list were Austrian marshaling yards at Innsbruck, Klagenfurt, and Sankt Veit.

Italy was again the focus on April 8, as more than five hundred B-24s and B-17s concentrated on the transportation system feeding into the Brenner Pass. Bridges, viaducts, and marshaling yards were bombed at or near Avisio, Brescia, Bressanone, Campo di Trens, Campodazzo, Fortezza, Gorizia, Mezzocorona, Ponte Gardena, Pordenone, and Vipiteno.

On April 9, the Fifteenth Air Force switched from strategic to tactical operations—the first time in many months—for one of its largest missions of the war. In cooperation with the British Eighth Army, 825 B-24s and B-17s attacked German army forward positions, including artillery sites, southeast of Bologna. The following day, the campaign continued with 648 heavy bombers attacking German positions and infantry defenses in a sector along the Santerno River.

On April 11, the Fifteenth Air Force returned to the strategic mission, sending 544 B-24s and B-17s against the Brenner Pass area. The idea was to isolate the German forces in Italy, who were seen as being on the verge of collapse. Specific locations were targeted at Bronzolo, Campo di Trens, Campodazzo, Goito, Ora, Osoppo, Padua, Ponte

What can be more idyllic than the sight of a natural metal B-17G resting under a blanket of newly fallen snow? The early weeks of January 1945 were, in fact, a quiet time for many USAAF Flying Fortress units. The cold, snowy weather over much of Europe cancelled many missions and gave the Third Reich an undeserved respite from the wrath of the Allied bombers. *USAAF via National Archives*

Gardena, and Vipiteno. The next day, the same lines of communications were targeted by more than 400 B-17s and B-24s attacking railroad bridges at Nervesa della Bataglia, Padua, and Ponte di Piave in Italy, as well as Sankt Veit in Austria, an ammunition dump at Malcontenta, and a supply dump at Peschiera del Garda. On April 14, 318 B-17s and B-24s targeted ammunition factories at Avigliana, Malcontenta, Palmanova, and Spilimbergo, and a motor transport depot at Osoppo.

April 15 marked a reversion to tactical operations and the largest Fifteenth Air Force mission of the year, as 830 B-17s and B-24s supported the ground advance of the U.S. Fifth Army by attacking German troops, gun positions, supply dumps, and maintenance installations on the roads leading north from Bologna. This mission continued for four days, although most of the bombers were

grounded because of weather on April 16. On April 17 and 18, 751 and 473 heavy bombers, respectively, continued to blast German positions to aid the forward momentum of the Fifth Army offensive near Bologna.

On April 19 and 20, strategic operations resumed, with an average of 660 B-17s and B-24s bombarding the rail lines between southern Germany and northern Italy. Specific targets included Avisio, Bischofshofen, Boara Pisani, Campo di Trens, Campodazzo, Fortezza, Grisolera, Innsbruck, Klagenfurt, Lienz, Linz, Ponte Gardena, Rattenberg, Rosenheim, and Vipiteno. On April 21, 240 B-17s and B-24s struck marshaling yards at Rosenheim in Germany and at Attnang-Puchheim, Spittal an der Drau, and Vocklabruck in Austria. By then, the names of smaller cities began appearing on target lists, as larger major targets had been all but decimated.

The battle damage suffered by this B-17G was terrible and deadly for the bombardier—if he was in the nose at the time—but a tremendous triumph for the pilot who brought her home. *USAAF via National Archives*

On April 23, the focus of action for 719 B-24s and B-17s was a series of bridges over the Brenta and Adige Rivers at Albaredo d'Adige, Badia, Bonavigo, Cavarzere, Legnano, Padua, and Zevio. The next day, another seven-hundred-plane effort targeted Italian bridges at Bassano del Grappa, Casarsa della Delizia, Fermata di Brondolo, Friola, Latisana, Spilimbergo, and Valbruna. Also on the target list were Austrian bridges at Arnoldstein, Drauburg, and Kolbnitz.

By then, the German ground forces south of the Alps were in a state of complete collapse, as was the industrial and transportation infrastructure of the Third Reich itself. The Fifteenth Air Force planners were scraping the bottom of the barrel for targets because there were few, other than a handful, targets of opportunity left to attack. The last mission against the railyard at Linz was flown on April 25 by 467 B-17s and B-24s.

On May 1, after having been grounded for four days by bad weather, twenty-seven B-17s bombed the rail station and marshaling yard at Salzburg. When they returned to their base, they closed the chapter. It was the last Fifteenth Air Force bombing mission of World War II.

Flak batteries open up as Flying Fortresses of the 95th Bombardment Group reach their target area in January 1945. Flak was light at this moment, but things would soon change. *USAAF via National Archives*

A gleaming natural metal B-17G heads for the target amid brilliant clear skies on January 17, 1945. On that date, one strike package of Flying Fortresses attacked port and refinery targets around Hamburg, while another worked over Reichsbahn facilities at Paderborn and Bielefeld. The vertical contrails may be those of escort fighters or those of Luftwaffe interceptors, whose favorite tactic was to slash through the bomber formations vertically with their guns blazing. *USAAF via National Archives*

THE EUROPEAN THEATER

As 1945 began, the massive attacks on the German industrial infrastructure wrought by B-17s and other Allied heavy bombers were devastating. In just six months, the output of petroleum-based materials had been cut in half and steel production was down 80 percent. The bombing had succeeded in tying down nearly 20 percent of the nonagricultural labor force, including two million workers engaged in debris clearance, reconstruction, and dispersal projects necessitated by the great air offensive.

Germany's raw material industries, its manufacturing industries, and its power supply were all dependent on coal. By January 1945, coal stocks were becoming exhausted and the condition of the Reichsbahn, Germany's national railroad, was in such a state that what little coal was left could hardly be shipped. Coal shipments in December 1944 were just 36 percent of their August level, and by March 1945, they would hardly be sufficient even for the needs of the Reichsbahn. At the beginning of 1945, the German economy was on the verge of collapse, and the Flying Fortresses were ready to push it over the edge.

The strategic offensive would not, however, resume in full force until the middle of January. It was a combination of bad weather and the need to cut off and cut up the German forces that had initiated the Battle of the Bulge in mid-December. As with the last two weeks of 1944, the first two weeks of 1945 found the Eighth Air Force devoting the majority of its resources to isolating the battlefield by targeting bridges, rail lines, marshaling yards, and other facilities directly involved in supplying enemy ground troops. The missions would be large. The Eighth was able to routinely launch about a thousand bombers each day as weather permitted. The strikes were usually organized into two waves each of B-17s and B-24s.

By that time in the war, the use of radar bombing systems permitted the aircraft to fly missions over the type of cloud cover that would have forced mission cancellations just a year earlier. This meant that heavy bombers could be launched nearly every day.

Ironically, even as Germany was on the ropes, it was the Luftwaffe—not the USAAF or RAF—that launched the first massive air campaign of 1945. The tide had turned in the Battle of the Bulge, and the Allied ground forces were pushing the German armies back into Germany. The Allies assumed that they had air superiority. Early on New Year's Day, however, more than eight hundred German fighters and fighter bombers conducted a massive sweep, codenamed *Bodenplatte* (Boilerplate), over Allied-held territory in northern Europe. Their objective was to destroy Allied tactical aircraft on the ground. Nearly five hundred Allied aircraft were hit, but the Luftwaffe itself lost nearly three hundred irreplaceable planes and pilots. The loss of Luftwaffe fighter strength would be to the gain of the Eighth Air Force bomber crews that were, even at that moment, streaming eastward high above the low-level air battle over the Bulge.

On New Year's Day, the Eighth Air Force armada consisted of 845 bombers and 725 fighters targeting petroleum and rail facilities across western Germany. Among them were 527 B-17s, oblivious to *Bodenplatte*, that bombed Dillenburg, Dollbergen, Gottingen, Hadamar, Kassel, Kirchbunden, Koblenz, Limburg, Magdeburg, Wetter, and Wetzlar. Only two Flying Fortresses were shot down. The three hundred Luftwaffe pilots lost in *Bodenplatte* would not be available to challenge the Allied bombers again.

The next day, 671 Flying Fortresses returned to blast communications centers, railyards, and other transportation facilities at Bad Kreuznach, Bitburg, Daun, Ehrang, Gerolstein, Kaiserslautern, Kyllburg, Lebach,

B-17Gs of the 532nd Bombardment Squadron of the 381st Bombardment Group en route to the target escorted by a P-51B "little friend." *USAAF via National Archives*

that lingers today. The debate centers on the Royal Air Force mixed high-explosive and incendiary attack on the nights of February 13 and 14. In contrast to the USAAF's daylight precision-bombing attacks against specific targets, the RAF conducted nighttime attacks against area targets using the tactic of carpet-bombing. In the case of the attack against Dresden, nearly eight hundred Avro Lancaster heavy bombers struck in two waves. Rather than hitting the city's industrial area, the RAF hit the Altstadt, or old city. It was the cultural heart of Dresden, filled with architecturally significant structures and a large civilian population. The ensuing firestorm killed a sizable number of people and is still used as an illustration of the horrors of strategic bombing. The Reich Propaganda Ministry

claimed a death toll of three hundred thousand, which clearly served the propaganda purpose. Exaggerated figures in excess of one hundred thousand are still mentioned. In fact, official German records of the time placed the number at less than twenty-two thousand. Had Adolf Hitler and the Nazis taken their own numbers as seriously as later peace activists have, they could have ended the war the following day by accepting the surrender terms offered by the Allies two years earlier. Instead, Hitler let his people endure the horrors of nearly three more months of the war he had started.

On February 14, 311 B-17s hit the marshaling yard at Dresden by daylight as part of an armada of 1,377 Eighth Air Force bombers and 962 fighters launched against enemy targets. The Dresden mission was accompanied by 124 additional Flying Fortresses that reached deep into Czechoslovakia to hit targets including Brux, Pilsen, and Prague. Another strike package of 514 Flying Fortresses attacked Bamberg, Chemnitz, Dulmen, the Eger Luftwaffe base, Hof, Sonneberg, Tachau, and Wesel. The next day, 211 B-17s bombed Dresden again, while 435 bombed Cottbus and 76 attacked other targets, including Munster and the Ems-Weser Canal. Dresden would be attacked by the USAAF twice more.

On February 16, 208 B-17s bombed Hamm's railyard, while 294 hit petroleum refineries at Dortmund and Nordstern, and 134 divided their attention among Langendreer, Meppen, Munster, Osnabruck, Rheine, and Wesel. The next day, weather caused numerous cancellations, but 260 Flying Fortresses got through to bomb Frankfurt and 71 hit Aschaffenburg, Giessen, and Hanau. On February 19, 796 B-17s attacked targets in Bochum, Dortmund, Gelsenkirchen, Haselunne, Munster, Osnabruck, Rheine, and Wesel.

The target on February 20 and 21 was the rail hub and adjacent tank factory in Nurnberg. It was plastered by a concentrated effort involving an incredible 1,662 Flying Fortress sorties over two days, while thirty-nine B-17s diverted to other targets. Only 5 Flying Fortresses were shot down during that massive campaign.

On February 22 and 23, the Eighth and Fifteenth Air Forces joined in Operation Clarion—an integrated effort to shut down the already devastated German transportation and communications network by attacking network hubs that had not previously received much attention. In a matter of two days, the Eighth launched a crushing 2,702 bomber sorties and 1,567 fighter sorties. The former included 1,882 Flying Fortress sorties, with minimal losses from the exhausted German defenses.

The list of targets struck by the B-17s during those 48 hours was like an encyclopedia of largely ignored German Reichsbahn rail hubs, as well as a few familiar targets. The sites included Aalen, Adelsberg, Ansbach, Bamberg, Crailsheim, Dannenberg, Donaueschingen, Ellingen, Freiburg, Grabow, Hafingen, Hildburghausen, Kitzingen, Klotze, Kobbelitz, Lichtenfels, Ludwigslust, Luneburg, Meiningen, Neumarkt, Neustadt, Nordlingen, Ottingen, Plauen, Reutlingen, Salzwedel, Schwabisch Hall, Schweinfurt, Schwenningen, Singen, Stendal, Treuchtlingen, Uelzen, Ulm, Villgen, Winterhausen, Wittenburg, Wittstock, Wurzburg, Zwickau, and Zwolle.

On February 24, 348 B-17s bombed petroleum refineries at Hamburg, and 200 hit the U-boat facilities at Bremen. Another 236 Flying Fortresses hit targets at Bremen, Brinkum, Minden, Osnabruck, Quackenbruck, and Wesel. The next day, the mix of industrial and rail targets for 309 B-17s included Friedrichshaffen, Kaufbeuren, Kempten, Kenzingen, Ludwigsfeldt, Neuburg, Rortwell, and Ulm, while 489 B-17s attacked targets in Munich.

On February 26, 781 Flying Fortresses hit the Reichsbahn stations at Alexanderplatz and Schlesischer in Berlin, while 5 bombed targets of opportunity. The following day, the Reichsbahn hub at Leipzig was

On Monday, February 26, 1945, the Eighth Air Force was able to launch more than 1,200 heavy bombers. Among them were these B-17Gs of the 94th Bombardment Group. In all, 418 Forts plastered the Alexanderplatz Reichsbahn station—the transit hub in central Berlin, within earshot of where Adolf Hitler lived out his final days. *USAAF via National Archives*

attacked by 717 Flying Fortresses, while 7 diverted to targets of opportunity. On the last day of the month, 739 B-17s mauled the Reichsbahn at Hagen, Kassel, Schwerte, and Soest.

As February gave way to March, railyards remained on the list as secondary, and occasionally primary, targets, but the focus gradually shifted from the rail network back to manufacturing facilities and the synthetic petroleum industry.

The new month began with 420 Flying Fortresses bombing the marshaling yard at Ulm, while 439 attacked rail targets at Bruchsal, Gottingen, Heidelberg, Heilbronn, Neckarsulm, and Reutlingen. On March 2, petroleum facilities took the lead as 868 B-17s attacked those and other targets at Bohlen, Chemnitz, Dresden, Köln, Rositz, Ruhland, and Saalfeld. The next day, 796 B-17s attacked refineries at Braunschweig, Dedenhausen, Dollbergen, Misburg, Nienhagen, and Ruhland, as well as the tank plant at Hannover and other targets at Chemnitz and Plauen.

On March 4 and 5, factories and petroleum facilities headed the list as 788 B-17 sorties attacked Ausbuch, Chemnitz, Fulda, Ingolstadt, Plauen, Reutlingen, Schwabmunchen, and Ulm—many of which were secondary targets because of the weather. Two days later, 250 Flying Fortresses attacked the benzine industrial solvent plants at Datteln and Castrop, while 71 hit targets at Siegen and Giessen. On March 8, the campaign against benzine production continued when 534 B-17s attacked factories at Bottrop, Dortmund, Essen, Huls, and Langendreer. About 400 Flying Fortresses hit other targets, including chemical plants at Frankfurt and Buer Scholren.

March 9 and 10 saw the Eighth Air Force strike factories and rail targets in attacks that included 1,692 B-17 sorties against Dortmund, Frankfurt, Hagen, Hamm, Kassel, Munster, Osnabruck, Rheine Schwerte, and Soest. The next day, 469 Flying Fortresses bombed a refinery in Hamburg, while 406 targeted the U-boat yard in Bremen. On March 12, rail targets headed the list as 388 B-17s attacked marshaling yards at Betzdorf, Dillenburg, Marburg, and Siegen. The Eighth Air Force returned refineries and factories to the head of the target list on March 14, when 876 Flying Fortresses attacked Bad Ostenhausen, Hameln, Hannover, Hildesheim, Lohne, Misburg, Nienhagen, Osnabruck, Seelze, and Wetzlar. The following day, 612 B-17s struck the Reichsbahn yard at Oranienburg, while 31 bombed Wittenberg, 13

A formation of Flying Fortresses from the 486th Bombardment Group crosses a coastal estuary en route to a target. *USAAF via National Archives*

bombed Stendal, and 15 diverted to other targets. Also on March 16, a combined armada of 276 B-17s and 308 B-24s bombed the command center of the Wehrmacht headquarters at Zossen, south of Berlin.

On March 17, 214 and 152 B-17s, respectively, bombed petroleum refineries at Ruhland and Bohlen, while 585 others hit refinery and factory targets at Altenburg, Bittefeld, Cottbus, Erfurt, Fulda, Jena, Molbis, and Plauen. The following day, a major effort against the German capital sent an incredible 916 Flying Fortresses to attack rail centers within Berlin in two waves, while 20 B-17s diverted to other targets. More than three hundred B-24s also hit Berlin on that day.

Flying Fortresses returned two days later to many of the industrial targets of March 17, as 436 bombed the factory complex at Plauen, 197 attacked the Karl Zeiss optics factory in Jena, and 79 attacked other targets, including Fulda. The port area at Hamburg, and its U-boat facilities, was the target on March 20 for 295 B-17s. The tank plant at Plauen was attacked again as a secondary target for 107 B-17s on March 21.

By that time, the Allied land armies were ready for their big push across the Rhine River and into the heart of Germany. Once again, the Eighth Air Force was tasked with attacking German forces behind the lines. The campaign began on March 21 with a concentrated effort against the Luftwaffe. The Allies did not want a repeat of *Bodenplatte* of New Year's Day. On March 21, 715 Flying

The U-boat pens and shipyards at Kiel and Hamburg were the primary targets of the day on April 4, 1945, as these 303rd Bombardment Group B-17Gs headed out. The Eighth Air Force launched more than 1,400 bombers that day. *USAAF via National Archives*

Fortresses hit Luftwaffe bases at Achmer, Hardorf, Hesepe, Hopsten, Rheine, Vorden, Wittmundhafen, and Zwischenahn. The next day, 208 B-17s attended to the Luftwaffe at Ahlhorn and Frankfurt, while 739 attacked troop concentrations at Barningholten, Bottrop, Dorsten, Feldhausen, Geresheim, Hinsbeck, Mulheim, Ratingen, and Westerholt.

As Allied forces poured eastward across the Rhine on March 23, the Eighth moved farther behind German lines to blast railyards in and around Coesfeld, Dortmund, Giesecke, Gladbeck, Haliger, Hechfeldt, Hengstey, Herdecke, Holzwickede, Marburg, Meschede, Recklinghausen, Schwerte, Siegen, and Westerholt with a thousand Flying Fortresses. The next day, the focus returned to the Luftwaffe, as more than eleven hundred B-17s in five strike packages bombed bases in Germany and the Netherlands such as Achmer, Enschede, Furstenau, Hesepe, Hopsten, Plantlunne, Rheine, Steenwijk, Varel, Varrelbusch, Vechta, Wittmundhafen, Ziegenhain, and Zwischenahn.

Poor weather over the following two days caused delays and cancellations in a planned return to strategic targets. But on March 26, 269 B-17s managed to bomb the tank plant at Plauen, while 62 others hit industrial targets at Markt Erlbach, Meiningen, Oelsnitz, Wurzburg, and Zeitz. Two days later, despite continued

inclement weather, 383 Flying Fortresses hit industrial targets in Berlin, while 465 attacked Hannover and 43 diverted to secondary targets.

Ten days after the last such Flying Fortress attack, the U-boat pens and adjacent facilities at Hamburg were attacked by 496 B-17s on March 30. In a second wave, 427 B-17s blasted the port and U-boat base at Bremen, while 32 Flying Fortresses attacked the U-boat bunker at nearby Farge with British deep-penetration bombs.

On March 31, industrial targets were the order of the day, as 503 B-17s attacked Aschersleben, Bad Berka, Brandenburg, Erfurt, Gotha, Halle, Leipzig, Salzwedel, Stendal, Weimar, and Zeitz.

The last month of the B-17's combat career began inauspiciously on April 2 with a mission against Luftwaffe bases in Denmark that had to be aborted because of heavy cloud cover. Over the following two days, the U-boat bases at Kiel were attacked by Flying Fortresses—for the first time since the summer of 1944—by a staggering 1,222 B-17 sorties. On April 4, 262 B-17s also attacked Luftwaffe bases and other targets at Dedelsdorf, Fassberg, Hoya, and Unterluss. The next day, a variety of targets, from Luftwaffe bases to Reichsbahn yards, were struck by 572 B-17s at or near Bayreuth, Furth, Grafenwohr, Ingolstadt, Nurnberg, and Weiden.

April 6 was a continuation of operations against the shriveling Reichsbahn rail network, as 321 B-17s hit the yards at Leipzig and 120 bombed the yards in Gera and

A B-17G of the 388th Bombardment Group unloads its ordnance over the target. *USAAF via National Archives*

Built by Lockheed-Vega at Burbank, this Block 40 B-17G served with the 447th Bombardment Group, where she was known as *A Bit-O-Lace*. The nose art of a reclining femme fatale was adapted from a character drawn by the legendary cartoonist Milton Caniff in his comic strip, *Male Call*. She is said to have been painted on the bomber by artist Nicholas Fingelly of the 447th's 709th Bombardment Squadron. Caniff was famous for his strip, *Terry and the Pirates*—of which *Male Call* was a spin-off circulated to service personnel in World War II—and for his postwar strip, *Steve Canyon*. *A Bit-O-Lace* is seen here with a dark green rudder that was retrofitted from another aircraft after she suffered severe tail damage on an April 4, 1945, mission. Nicknamed *Miss Lace,* she completed eighty-three missions and was flown back to Kingman, Arizona, after the war and scrapped in about 1947. *USAAF via National Archives*

In this marvelous photograph shot at a very high shutter speed, we can see the contrails forming as the high temperatures of the powerful Wright Cyclones make contact with the frigid air at the operational altitude of these Flying Forts. *Author collection*

Halle. Fuel depots and Luftwaffe facilities were added to the target list the next day, and 934 Flying Fortresses clouded the skies over Buchen, Fassberg, Gustrow, Hitzacker, Kaltenkirchen, Kohlenbissen, Lundeburg, Neumunster, Parchim, Salzwedel, Schwerin, Uelzen, and Wesendorf.

With the industrial districts in most of Germany's major cities effectively destroyed, the Eighth Air Force had gradually turned its attention to smaller cities to which factories had been dispersed in an effort to protect them from large raids by the heavy bombers.

On April 8 and 9, the target list continued to be a mixed bag of depots, railyards, and Luftwaffe facilities, as 1,723 B-17 sorties hammered Derben, Eger, Furstenfeldbruck, Grafenwohr, Halberstadt, Hof, Ingolstadt, Neuburg, Oberpfaffenhofen, Plauen, the Riem Luftwaffe base near Munich, Schafstadt, Schleissheim, and Wolfratshausen. The following day, the focus was on Luftwaffe bases, as 929 B-17s attacked Brandenburg, Burg-Bei-Magdeburg, Neuruppin, Oranienburg, Stendal, Zerbst, and the Rechlin Luftwaffe experimental base near Berlin. Between the B-17s and B-24s that also raided Luftwaffe bases on that date, the USAAF officially reported that 335 enemy aircraft were destroyed on the ground.

On April 11, depots, railyards, and industrial targets at Donauworth, Freiham, Ingolstadt, Kraiburg, Landshut, and Treuchtlingen were attacked by 933 Flying Fortresses. The following day, Friday the thirteenth, was an unlucky one for Neumunster—212 Flying Fortresses bombed the Reichsbahn facilities there—and for the crews of two B-17s that were shot down.

During the summer of 1944, as the Allies liberated France, the German garrisons at a number of locations along the west and northwest coasts retreated into heavily fortified redoubts. Because the fortresses were essentially impregnable, the Allies had chosen not to assault them. The German troops were surrounded and cut off. They couldn't conduct offensive operations, so the Allies just sealed them up and bypassed them. With the war closing in on its final three weeks, the Eighth Air Force was called upon to soften up the forts for the final surrender. To that end, 1,414 B-17 sorties and 656 B-24 sorties were flown on April 14 and 15 against Pointe Grave, Pointe Coubre, and Royan, near the mouth of the River Gironde.

On April 16, the B-17 force was back over Germany, with 447 Flying Fortresses attacking bridges and railyards at Platting, Regensburg, and Straubing. The next three days would involve deep penetrations into southern Germany and Czechoslovakia by 1,357 B-17 sorties that attacked Aussig (Usti), Dresden, Elsterwerda, Falkenberg, Freising, Karlsbad (Karlovy Vary), Kollin, Pilsen, Pirna, Rosenheim, Roundnice, and Traunstein.

On April 20, as Hitler turned fifty-six in the Berlin bunker that would soon be his death site, the Eighth Air Force bombed targets to the north and south of his doomed capital. Among the bombers in action that day were 583 B-17s attacking Brandenburg, Nauen, Neuruppin, Oranienburg, Seddin, Treuenbrietzen, and Wustermark. The next day, a wave of 111 B-17s bombed the Munich railyard, while another wave of 218 Flying Fortresses hit Ingolstadt and Landsberg.

On April 25, as American GIs and Soviet Red Army troops made contact along the Elbe River west of Berlin, the Eighth Air Force launched its last combat missions of World War II. A total of 589 bombers and 486 fighters took off from England on that final operation. Of them, 276 B-17s attacked the Luftwaffe base and the Skoda armament works in Pilsen, Czechoslovakia. There were 6 B-17s lost on the final mission—2 from the 398th Bombardment Group (Heavy) and 1 each from the 92nd, 303rd, 305th, and 384th Groups. The latter unit had the distinction of being the last Flying Fortress outfit to bomb an enemy target.

World War II in Europe was over, hastened by the potent destructive power of the B-17. As Germany's Armaments Minister Albert Speer wrote in his report on March 15, 1945, "The German economy is heading for an inevitable collapse within four to six weeks."

There had been a phenomenal increase in the weight of attack that could be brought against the enemy. In 1940, the Royal Air Force started out with an average monthly delivery of 1,128 tons, which increased to almost 6,000 tons in 1942 when the U.S. Army Air Forces joined the offensive. In 1943, the monthly delivery was 26,000 tons; in 1944, it was 130,000 tons, and in 1945, it reached 170,000 tons.

Even if the final land victories that carried the Allied armies across the Rhine and the Oder had not taken place, armament production would have come to a virtual standstill by May 1945. The actual collapse had occurred before the lack of means would have rendered further resistance physically impossible. As Speer had pointed out, the German armies, with no ammunition or motive power, would almost certainly have had to cease fighting by July.

This huge number of Flying Fortresses, unmarked with unit insignia, had reached England shortly before the German surrender. Most would never see action against the Third Reich. Many were returned to the United States as a first step in redeployment to the Pacific Theater, but Japan also surrendered before the Eighth Air Force could begin operations there.
USAAF via National Archives

THE FINAL ACTIONS OF THE
B-17 IN WORLD WAR II

Throughout the final months of the war, B-17s and B-24s had routinely flown leaflet-dropping missions over German-occupied territory and areas in which Allied armies were operating. It was considered to be the best way for SHAEF to communicate directly with civilians and with German troops who might be induced to lay down their arms rather than to risk their lives in Hitler's lost cause. After the Eighth Air Force concluded combat operations, the leaflet missions continued. During the final two days of April, as the ground war sputtered to an end, B-17s flew fourteen leaflet-dropping sorties over France, Germany, and the Netherlands. Such missions would continue through May 8, 1945.

When May began, B-17s were tasked with a campaign to drop food to hungry civilians in the recently liberated Netherlands. During the first three days of the month, 1,180 B-17 sorties dropped 4.6 million pounds of supplies to the people in cities such as Den Haag, Hilversum,

Rotterdam, and Utrecht, as well as at the Dutch airports—all former Luftwaffe bases—at Alkmaar and Schiphol, near Amsterdam. Between May 5 and May 7, 1,012 Flying Fortress sorties dropped an additional 3.7 million pounds.

On May 7, General Alfred Jodl, chief of operations for Germany's Wehrmacht, formally surrendered to General Eisenhower at SHAEF headquarters in Reims, France, and World War II was finally over in Europe. The last B-17 operations involved twenty-seven leaflet-dropping sorties on May 7 and 8 over Germany.

In Italy, the Fifteenth Air Force flew its last offensive mission on May 1, nearly a week after the last such Eighth Air Force operation. After that date, the Fifteenth's B-17s conducted reconnaissance missions for several days, until the Eighth and Fifteenth officially stood down on May 8. The Fifteenth was formally deactivated on September 15, 1945.

As previously planned, the Eighth Air Force was to pull up stakes at its bases in England as soon as Germany was defeated and make the transition to the Pacific Theater for the final offensive against Japan. There, it would join the Twentieth Air Force as a key component of the U.S. Army Strategic Air Forces (USASTAF) in the Pacific. Equipped exclusively with B-29 Superfortress very-heavy bombers, the Twentieth had been conducting a sustained air offensive against Japan since October 1944 and the Eighth would augment its power. The distance from Okinawa to Japan's industrial heartland was roughly equivalent to the distance from England to the targets in Germany to which the Eighth's B-17s had been flying. Having withdrawn them from the Pacific in 1943 to concentrate their weight against the Third Reich, the USAAF sent the Flying Fortresses back to fight Japan.

On May 9, even as the armistice with Germany was just taking effect, the first Eighth Air Force squadrons began to depart from England, heading west via the continental United States. Personnel left by ship, while aircraft flew south to staging bases at Istres in southern France and Casablanca in French Morocco. There, they began returning home via Africa and South America—the shortest crossing of the Atlantic. In the following eight weeks, half of the Eighth Air Force personnel strength would be redeployed to the United States from England.

On July 16, 1945, as the United States tested its first nuclear weapon in the New Mexico desert, the headquarters of the Eighth Air Force was officially relocated from the European Theater to Okinawa.

By August 5, the headquarters of the first Eighth Air Force groups assigned to the Pacific arrived in Okinawa, but the B-17s were still in the pipeline. The next day, the Twentieth Air Force conducted its first nuclear strike on Japan. Three days later, as the Eighth Air Force continued to transfer personnel and equipment westward across the United States toward its planned new home on Okinawa, the Twentieth Air Force dropped the second and last nuclear weapon used in World War II. The Twentieth flew its last offensive B-29 mission against Japan on August 14, and the following day, Japan announced that its emperor would accept Allied surrender terms. The official surrender took place on September 2, 1945, in Tokyo Bay.

No operational Eighth Air Force B-17s had reached the Pacific when Japan capitulated, so that chapter of the combat career of the Flying Fortress would go unwritten.

The Eighth Air Force airmen, along with their counterparts in the Fifteenth Air Force and in the Pacific Theater, are the true heroes of the Flying Fortress story in World War II. *USAAF via National Archives*

This Flying Fortress was part of the last block of B-17Gs built by Lockheed-Vega in Burbank in 1945. It is seen here with turrets removed in July 1946 during the Operation Crossroads nuclear weapons tests at Bikini Atoll in the Pacific. The Flying Fortresses were not actually used to drop nuclear weapons, but as QB-17G drones, which flew into the mushroom clouds to sample the air, and as DB-17Gs to remotely control the QB-17Gs. *USAAF via National Archives*

Nine-O-Nine is a fully restored B-17G owned and operated by the Collings Foundation of Stow, Massachusetts. The aircraft was built during World War II, but never served in combat. The bomber is now painted in the markings of the original *Nine-O-Nine*, which flew 140 missions with the 323rd Bombardment Squadron of the 91st Bombardment Group without an abort or loss of a crewman. The Collings Foundation was founded in 1979 to organize and support living history events. Since 1989, a major focus of the foundation has been the Veterans' Wings of Freedom Tour, which showcases a fully restored Consolidated B-24J Liberator, as well as this B-17G. Note the historically correct forty-eight star American flag. *Bill Yenne*

EPILOGUE

THE FLYING FORTRESS AFTER WORLD WAR II

WHEN WORLD WAR II ENDED, the B-17's combat career was essentially over. The last combat missions were flown by three Flying Fortresses that found their way to Israel after World War II. Those B-17s flew about two dozen missions with the fledgling Israeli air force during the 1948 War of Independence, including one high-altitude raid on Cairo.

Meanwhile, the USAAF had imploded. Heavy bombers were being scrapped as fast as possible, as the USAAF imagined that its future would involve deterring enemies with nuclear weapons delivered by B-29s. At the end of 1944, the USAAF possessed 4,419 B-17s and 5,678 B-24s equipping seventy-three heavy bombardment groups, and 942 B-29s equipping twenty-four very-heavy bombardment groups. There were a total of 242 groups. A year later, there were 109 groups, including seventy heavy bombardment groups with 1,400 B-17s and 1,103 B-24s, as well as twenty-eight very-heavy bombardment groups with 2,157 B-29s. At the end of 1946, the total number of USAAF groups of all types fell to fifty-two, with the last two heavy bomber groups deactivated in November 1946. The 512

Flying Fortresses that remained were relegated to second-line duties.

In the late 1940s and early 1950s, the USAAF (U.S. Air Force after September 1947) used Flying Fortresses designated as QB-17 drones to sample radiation during nuclear tests in the South Pacific and as targets for new air defense guided missiles, including those of the Nike family. About a dozen USAAF B-17Gs were equipped with lifeboats to serve as search-and-rescue aircraft. They were designated as B-17H, and as SB-17G after 1947. Nearly fifty B-17s that were transferred to the U.S. Navy under the patrol designation PB-1 served in a variety of roles, including coastal patrol, until about 1955.

Small numbers of Flying Fortresses served in non-combat roles or on patrol duty with the air forces of Brazil, Canada, the Dominican Republic, and Portugal, but the duties were terminated by the 1960s. The Swiss government operated a few B-17s that had been interned during the war when they made emergency landings in Switzerland. The governments of Denmark and France each operated a single Flying Fortress as an executive transport in the 1940s. Both the Nationalist Chinese

This Lockheed-Vega-built Flying Fortress served the Air Weather Service as an SB-17G rescue aircraft in Alaska during the 1950s. *E. Van Houten via David Menard*

(Taiwan) government and the American CIA operated B-17s for clandestine surveillance missions in Asia until the late 1950s.

B-17s that were sold to civilian operators were used for myriad tasks for four decades, including executive transportation, airline survey flights, and attacking forest fires with borate.

As noted earlier, the Flying Fortress became a film star during the war in William Wyler's documentary *Memphis Belle: A Story of a Flying Fortress*. After the war, the B-17 and its combat career continued to be immortalized by Hollywood directors in such films as Sam Wood's *Command Decision* (1948), starring Clark Gable and Walter Pidgeon, and Philip Leacock's *The War Lover* (1962), with Steve McQueen and Robert Wagner. Henry King's 1949 Flying Fortress film, *Twelve O'Clock High*, with Gregory Peck, became a television series that ran for three years beginning in 1964. More recently, there was Michael Caton-Jones' 1990 fictional adaptation of Wyler's *Memphis Belle*, starring Matthew Modine, Harry Connick Jr., and five surviving Flying Fortresses.

By the dawn of the twenty-first century, more than three dozen B-17s survived, including about a dozen in flyable condition that were still active on the air show circuit. These relics provide a fitting reminder of one of history's greatest aircraft types. Even when the last birds no longer fly, the memory of the service provided by the B-17 Flying Fortress will live on forever.

One of the last B-17Gs still in the inventory of the U.S. Air Force is pictured at San Francisco International Airport in the 1950s. The lack of markings suggests that this may have been one of many surplus B-17s that were used for clandestine (and still-secret) operations early in the Cold War. *Author collection*

Photographed by the author in 1980, the B-17G now known as *Virgin's Delight* is seen here on the tarmac at Castle Air Force Base in California, with Boeing KC-135s in the distance. This actual aircraft was built in 1944 but never sent overseas. Now the property of the Castle Air Museum, she is painted in the colors of the original *Virgin's Delight*, which served with the Eighth Air Force 94th Bombardment Group, commanded by Colonel Frederick Walker Castle, the namesake of Castle Air Force Base. He commanded the 94th from June 1943 to April 1944, when he was promoted to brigadier general and given command of the 4th Combat Wing. He was killed in action over France on December 24, 1944, while leading 2,034 bombers and 853 fighters in the largest strategic air attack in history. Castle's heavily damaged B-17 exploded as he was trying to keep it level so that the crew could bail out. Six men survived, and Castle was posthumously awarded the Medal of Honor. The aircraft seen here has since had its B-17G chin turret reattached. *Bill Yenne*

INDEX

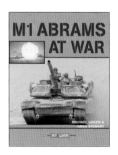

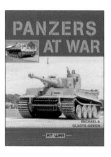
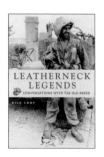
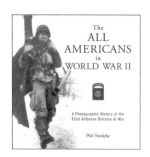
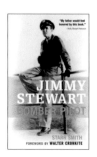